D0601966

Choosing God's Way to see and share

V. GILBERT BEERS
RONALD A. BEERS

VICTOR BOOKS a division of SP Publications, Inc.
WHEATON, ILLINOIS 60187

Offices also in
Whitby, Ontario, Canada
Amersham-on-the-Hill, Bucks, England

ARTISTS

Ann Iosa
Robert Korta
Luciana Peters
Blanche Sims
Suzanne Snider

Second printing, 1983

Library of Congress Catalog Card Number: 83-060339
ISBN: 0-88207-819-4

Manufactured in the United States of America

To Parents and Teachers

Of course you want your child to choose God's way. There are so many ways that compete for his or her mind and heart, and some may seem quite appealing to your child. But as Christians you and I have discovered that God's way is the only way that will give your child a truly happy life.

Have you ever asked what specifically you want your child to do in choosing God's way for his life? This book focuses on 28 ways to please God in daily life. Each is a choice. Your child can choose to give or to keep, to be friendly or unfriendly, to forgive or to hold a grudge, to be honest or dishonest, to be kind or unkind, to obey or disobey. The choices he or she makes are important in pleasing God or in not pleasing Him. They are important also in pleasing or in not pleasing parents and teachers.

In the following 4-page guide, these 28 ways are listed alphabetically by key word—honest, kind, leader, listen, and love. Following each key word are stories and page numbers, where that way is both pictured and described.

Like MY PICTURE BIBLE TO SEE AND SHARE, this book is a Read-to-Me Picture Book for the preschool and early elementary child. You will find 174 colorful paintings, each dramatizing a true-to-life situation which will help boys and girls choose God's way. Each picture, and its accompanying picture reading feature, helps your child discover how to choose God's way to honesty, love, patience, thankfulness, or one of the other 24 ways.

A short section called WHAT DO YOU SEE? helps your child develop "discovery power," finding the little things he may ordinarily pass by. Another short question section called A TIME TO SHARE provides questions you will want to ask your child. This activity will help your child share thoughts with you, and will be a sharing time, bearing special fruit as you and your child develop a closer relationship in choosing God's way.

V. Gilbert Beers

Table of Contents

Choosing God's Way

a guide to 28 important ways your child can choose to live for God

Choosing to be
RESPONSIBLE

Choosing to
SHARE

Choosing to be
SORRY

Choosing to be
THANKFUL

Choosing to
TRUST

Choosing to tell the
TRUTH

Choosing to be
UNSELFISH

Let Me Swing and Sing and Laugh

Choosing to be HAPPY

Isn't it fun to swing? This boy and girl think so. Higher and higher they go. They laugh. They sing. And they talk together about good things. You can tell they are happy, can't you? But do you see the boy and girl behind them? They aren't happy, are they? Look at them argue and fight. They could be swinging and laughing and singing and talking. But they aren't. Which boy and girl do you think will have a better day?

A TIME TO SHARE

1. *What are the boy and girl doing together?*
2. *What are the boy and girl behind them doing?*
3. *Which would you rather be right now? Why?*
4. *Which pleases Jesus more? Why?*

WHAT DO YOU SEE?

Which boy and girl are happy? Which are not happy? How can you tell?

Shh, Kitty! Father Is Praying

Choosing to PRAY

Look at kitty under the girl's chair. She is rolling around and around. Thump, bump, bump, thump! "Shh, kitty! Father is praying!" That's what the girl wants to tell kitty. The girl wants to hear what Father says. He is talking to Jesus. He is thanking Jesus for their good food. He is glad Jesus has given them this good food. That's why he is saying thank You. Don't you think that's a good thing to do?

WHAT DO YOU SEE?
Can you find the six bowls of food? What do you think each one is? How many knives, forks, spoons, and dishes can you find? Point to each one.

A TIME TO SHARE

1. *Why is Father praying?*
2. *Why not just eat? Why pray?*
3. *Who is Father talking to?*

Hold My Hand and Don't Let Go

Choosing to TRUST

People, people, people! Some are coming here, and others are going there. When you get a lot of people in one place, it is called a crowd. Do you see the crowd in the picture? How would you like to be lost in a crowd? How would you like to be all alone, without Father or Mother or a friend with you? It would be scary, wouldn't it? That's why this girl is glad to be with her father. That's why she is holding onto her father's hand. She trusts her father to take her to the right place. She trusts her father to take her home again.

A TIME TO SHARE

1. *Look at the girl's hand and her father's hand. What are they doing?*
2. *Who else in this picture would she trust as much as her father?*
3. *How do you show that you trust your parents?*

WHAT DO YOU SEE?

How many people do you see in this picture? How many of these people are helping the girl find her way? What do you see that tells you the girl trusts her father?

Please Let Me Help You

Choosing to be HELPFUL

Oh! Oh! That lady has dropped a package. How can she ever bend down and pick it up? Her arms are filled with other packages. But here is a girl who wants to be helpful. She does not have packages in her arms. So she can bend down easier than the lady. This is a time for "please let me help you." It is also a time for "thank you, what a good helper." That's why Mother is smiling.

WHAT DO YOU SEE?

How many people are smiling? Why should the girl smile? Why should the lady with the packages smile? Why should Mother smile?

A TIME TO SHARE

1. *What is the girl doing?*
2. *Why is she doing this?*
3. *Think of some ways you can be helpful.*
4. *Will you do one of them today?*

I Love You, Mother

Choosing to show LOVE

Mother is sick. That's why she is in bed. When we are sick it is hard to get up and fix our own breakfast, isn't it? We need someone who loves us to help. Do you see why Mother is smiling? She knows now that her girl wants to do something special for her. Isn't that a wonderful way to say, "I love you, Mother"?

WHAT DO YOU SEE?
What is the girl wearing? Why does that tell you she has fixed breakfast? What do you see on the tray? Can you tell what time it is?

A TIME TO SHARE

1. *What is wrong with Mother?*
2. *Why does she need help?*
3. *How is the girl showing love to her mother?*

Thank You, God

Choosing to be THANKFUL

Genesis 8:15—9:17

Have you gone on a long trip in your car? You were glad to stop and rest, weren't you? These people have been on a long trip. They have been inside a big boat for many days. They could not go outside. There was nothing but water around the boat. Each day these people worked hard inside the boat. There were many animals to feed and stalls to clean. But now at last the water has gone away. The people can go outside the boat. They are thankful that the boat kept them safe on the water. But they are also thankful that they can come out of the boat. Do you see how they are thanking God? You thank God in other ways, don't you?

A TIME TO SHARE

1. *What are these people doing?*
2. *What are they saying to God?*
3. *How do you tell God you are thankful?*
4. *Have you thanked God today?*

WHAT DO YOU SEE?

Do you see the big boat? Is it too big to go on a river or lake you know about? Can you find the stone altar? Noah and his family burned meat on this altar. It was their way to say, "Thank You, God."

Wait!

Choosing to OBEY

Wait! The policeman doesn't want you to cross the street just now. Perhaps a car is coming. It may be coming fast. It could hurt you. The children are happy to wait. They know the policeman is their friend. They know he has a good reason to tell them to wait. But look! Two of the children are not waiting. They are not obeying the policeman. Do you see them running across the street when they should be waiting with the others? They should obey the policeman, shouldn't they?

A TIME TO SHARE

1. *What would you like to tell the children who are obeying?*
2. *What would you like to tell the two who are not?*
3. *Do you like to obey? Why? Who does it please?*

WHAT DO YOU SEE?

How many children do you see waiting? How many are not waiting? How do you know the man in the street is a policeman? Point to some things that tell you.

WHAT DO YOU SEE?
How many boys and girls are in this parade? What else do you see in the parade? What tells you that these boys and girls are having fun?

This Way!

Choosing to be a LEADER

Here's a happy parade, isn't it? Can't you hear the horn tooting and the drum booming? Listen! What else do you hear in this parade? These boys and girls are having fun, aren't they? Around and around they go. But where are they going? Who are they following? Do you think they are following the boy with the cymbals? What about the boy with the drum? They are following the boy with the horn, aren't they? He is the leader. Wherever he goes, the rest will go. Do you like to be a leader?

A TIME TO SHARE

1. *Who is leading this parade?*
2. *Who is following?*
3. *Do you like to lead? Do you like to follow sometimes?*
4. *Before you lead, know where you are going!*

Stop Fidgeting and Fussing

Choosing to be PATIENT

Here are two brothers. They are late for the ball game, and they are supposed to play. But do you see one brother there with his father? What is he doing? He doesn't look as if he is fidgeting and fussing, does he? Father is doing all he can to fix that tire and get to the game. Now look at the other brother. He is not helping at all. Instead, he is standing there, fidgeting and fussing. Do you think that will help to get the tire fixed? Do you think it will help them to get to the ball game faster? What will? Which brother is being more patient? Which brother is pleasing Father more?

WHAT DO YOU SEE?

What is Father doing with that car? Why does that keep them from getting to the ball game on time? Which brother is being more patient?

A TIME TO SHARE

1. *Look at the brother standing up. Why do you think he is not being patient?*
2. *How does the other brother look different?*
3. *Which brother would you like to be like? Why?*
4. *Which will you be like today? How?*

Are You Doing What You Should?

Choosing to be RESPONSIBLE

You can almost hear that vacuum cleaner running, can't you? How does it sound? But Mother doesn't mind helping her girl clean this room. She is glad because her girl is doing her part too. Do you see what she is doing? Look at that dustcloth go. She is even dusting under her lamp. This girl is learning to be responsible. She began to clean her room without Mother telling her. Mother was so happy that she got the vacuum cleaner and began helping her. Do you think that is why both of them look so happy?

WHAT DO YOU SEE?

Whose room is this? How do you know? Why do you think this is not Mother's room? Can you point to some kinds of things you see in your room? Do you see the girl's kitten? Does he look like yours?

A TIME TO SHARE

1. *Why do you think the girl is so happy?*
2. *Why do you think Mother is so happy?*
3. *Are you happy when you do what you should? Why? Why does that make Mother happy too?*

Here Come Those Men Again

Choosing to CONTROL YOURSELF

Genesis 26:12-33

Here come those bad men again! Do you see them? Poor Isaac! He and his friends have just dug a well. They are putting the stones around the top. But these bad men will take the well from Isaac. They did this before. Isaac's friends wanted to fight. Isaac wanted to fight too. But he knew that it is sometimes better not to fight. When the men came before, Isaac let them take the well. He will do that again. Then the men will stop bothering him. They know that he will not fight. Sometimes we want to fight when people bother us. Later we are glad that we didn't.

A TIME TO SHARE

1. *What is Isaac doing?*
2. *What will those bad men do now?*
3. *Why doesn't Isaac fight them?*
4. *When should you not fight?*

WHAT DO YOU SEE?

There are two groups of men. What group is Isaac's group? How do you know? Which men are the bad men who will take his well?

What Is He Doing?

Choosing to be GOOD

Do you see what that boy is doing? He should be reading his book, shouldn't he? The boy in front of him is reading his book. He is being good because he is doing what he should. People who do what they should are being good. People who are doing things they shouldn't do are not being good. What would you like to say to that boy with the rubber band? What would you like to tell him about being good?

A TIME TO SHARE

1. *Which boy is being good?*
2. *How do you know he is being good?*
3. *Which boy is not being good?*
4. *How do you know he is not being good?*

WHAT DO YOU SEE?

What do you see that tells you this is a school? What do you see on the wall? Where are the boys sitting? What is on their desks?

Who Is at the Cookie Jar?

Choosing to be HONEST

Oh! Oh! Do you see what that girl is doing? Her mother does not see her, does she? You know that because of the way she is watching her mother. Even her dog is watching! This girl is doing something wrong, isn't she? She is taking a cookie without asking her mother first. If she asked, her mother might give her a cookie. Then both of them would be happy. But what do you think the girl's mother will say if she looks up now? What do you think she may do to the girl? Taking things without asking is not honest, is it? God is sad when we are not honest. Our parents are sad too. And that makes us sad, doesn't it?

A TIME TO SHARE

1. *What is the girl doing?*
2. *Why is that wrong?*
3. *Why is she not being honest?*
4. *What should she do to please her mother and to please God?*

WHAT DO YOU SEE?

Look at the girl's eyes. Why is she looking that way? Look at the dog's eyes. Why is he looking that way? Now look at Mother's eyes. What is she doing? Do you think Mother will keep on smiling if she looks up and sees what the girl is doing? Why not?

Family Love

Choosing to show LOVE

Now there are some people who love each other. You can see that, can't you? You can see that they like to do things together. They are not doing these things because they should. They are doing them because they are having fun. Family love is fun. Don't you think Father knows that? Don't you think Mother knows that? Don't you think their girl knows that? You know that too, don't you?

A TIME TO SHARE

1. *Why should families do things together?*
2. *How is that choosing to show love?*
3. *What special things do you like to do with Mother or Father?*

WHAT DO YOU SEE?

What are Father and the girl doing together? What is Mother doing? Do you think she is having fun watching Father and their girl?

She Did It!

Choosing to tell the TRUTH

Crash! Everyone heard that jar fall. Mother heard it, didn't she? It didn't take her long to come here to see what happened. But look at that girl. She is pointing to her sister. "She did it!" That's what she is telling her mother. But do you think Mother believes it? Do you think Mother knows her girl is not telling the truth?

A TIME TO SHARE

1. *Why is the girl pointing to her sister?*
2. *What do you think Mother is saying?*
3. *Who is pleased when we tell the truth?*

WHAT DO YOU SEE?

How do you think that girl broke the jar? Why do you think Mother didn't break it? Why do you think the girl in the chair didn't do it?

Give Your Money to Jesus

Choosing to GIVE

Here's a happy Sunday School class! The three girls in the back row are smiling. The boy putting his money in the collection basket is smiling. He is happy to give his money to Jesus. The boy who is reaching out to take the basket is smiling too. He is ready to give his money to Jesus. But look! The boy next to the teacher is not smiling. He does not look happy at all. Do you see him still holding his money? The offering basket went by, and he did not put his money in. He is keeping it. The boy does not want to give his money. Perhaps that is the reason he is not smiling. What do you think would make him happy?

WHAT DO YOU SEE?

How many coins do you see? Which coin is going into the offering basket? Which will go in soon? Which should have gone in but didn't?

A TIME TO SHARE

1. *Why is the one boy so sad?*
2. *Why are the other boys happy?*
3. *Why are you happier when you give than when you keep?*
4. *How does this money help?*

Someone Is With Me

Choosing to have COURAGE
1 Samuel 17

Oh, no! Look at the giant. He is almost as big as two men. Do you see his sword and spear? How can poor David fight this man? Do you see what David has? It is only a little sling and some rocks. How can David win? Who will help him? Don't you think David should be afraid? But David isn't afraid. He knows Someone special is helping him. God is there with David. God is much bigger than the giant. So God will help David win this fight. That's why David is not afraid.

A TIME TO SHARE

1. *Does the giant think he will win? Why?*
2. *Does David think he will win? Why?*
3. *When God is with you, why should you not be afraid?*

WHAT DO YOU SEE?

How would you feel if you had to fight this giant? Point to some things on the giant that would make you afraid.

Are You Following?

Choosing to FOLLOW

"That's right. The answer is 12. Now for the next problem. Are you following me?" Teacher doesn't like it if you don't follow what he is saying, does he? One of these boys is following the teacher, isn't he? But look at that other boy. How can he follow what the teacher says if he is playing with that cube? The boy knows he is not following the teacher. The teacher knows too. You can see by the way he is looking at the boy. What do you think the teacher will say now?

WHAT DO YOU SEE?

Look at the boy's paper. Is that what the teacher wrote on the board? He wasn't following the teacher very well, was he?

A TIME TO SHARE

1. *What is the boy with the cube doing?*
2. *What should he be doing?*
3. *Why should we follow what our teacher says?*
4. *Why should we follow what our parents say?*

Come, Play with Us

Choosing to be FRIENDLY

Those three girls by the house are having fun, aren't they? But what about this poor girl with the hearts on her shirt? She doesn't look as if she is having much fun, does she? It isn't much fun to stand alone and watch others play, is it? But look! One of the girls is calling to her. Do you think she is asking this girl to come and play? Do you think this will make the lonely girl happy? That's a wonderful way to be friendly, isn't it?

WHAT DO YOU SEE?

Three girls have smiles on their faces. Can you find them? One girl does not have a smile on her face. Can you find her? Will she have a smile when she goes to play with the others?

A TIME TO SHARE

1. *Have you ever been lonely?*
2. *How did it feel when someone was friendly?*
3. *Do you know someone who is lonely?*
4. *Will you be a good friend by being friendly?*

I Will Stay with My Friend

Choosing to be LOYAL

Look at that poor dog in the basket! He is sick. He has been sick all day. Now it is late at night, and the boy should be in bed. But he doesn't want to go to bed. He wants to stay there with his dog. He knows his dog would stay with him if he were sick. So the boy waits and hopes that his dog will get better. Don't you think the poor dog is glad that his friend is loyal?

A TIME TO SHARE

1. *Why does the boy look sleepy?*
2. *Why doesn't he go to bed?*
3. *How is the boy showing that he is loyal?*
4. *What are some other ways to be loyal?*

WHAT DO YOU SEE?

How do you know that it is late at night? What does the clock tell you? What do the boy's eyes tell you?

Who Are You?

Choosing to tell the TRUTH
Genesis 27:1-29

Look at that man kneeling there by his father. That is Jacob. He wants his father to give him a special gift. Jacob's father Isaac had planned to give this special gift to Jacob's brother Esau. The father is blind and old. He cannot see Jacob. So Jacob put on that hairy stuff. He is pretending to be Esau, who has hair on his arms and neck. Jacob is lying to his father. He is telling his father that he is Esau. Poor Father. He believes Jacob. So he gives Esau's special gift to Jacob. How do you think Father will feel when he learns the truth?

WHAT DO YOU SEE?
Do you see the goat hair tied to Jacob's arms and neck? When Father feels this he thinks he is touching Esau. Esau has lots of hair on his arms and neck.

A TIME TO SHARE

1. *Who is Jacob pretending to be?*
2. *Why is he doing this?*
3. *Why will Father be hurt when he hears the truth? Why should we always tell the truth?*

Will You Forgive Me?

Choosing to FORGIVE

Do you see something wrong? Do you see why the girl is crying? Mother sees! Mother is sad because the girl broke one of her good dishes. But she is not crying. She is putting her arms around the girl. She sees that her girl is sorry that she broke the dish. So Mother is forgiving her. Aren't you glad when someone forgives you for doing something wrong? Do you remember to forgive others when they do something wrong?

A TIME TO SHARE

1. *Why is the girl crying?*
2. *Why is Mother hugging her?*
3. *Do you ever ask Mother or Father to forgive you?*
4. *Do you ever ask God to forgive you?*

WHAT DO YOU SEE?

How many pieces of the plate can you count? It is really broken, isn't it? Do you see the other dishes that are not broken? Point to them.

Someone to Help

Choosing to be KIND

That man wants to cross the street. But he is blind. He does not have a dog to help him cross the street. He does not have a friend to help him either. Do you see the children across the street? Are they helping the blind man? Do you see the mother and father across the street? Are they helping the blind man? He needs someone to help him. Now look! Do you see the boy with the blind man? What do you think he is saying? He wants to be kind. He wants to help the blind man across the street. You would do that if you could, wouldn't you?

A TIME TO SHARE

1. *What does the blind man want to do?*
2. *Which people are not helping him?*
3. *Which one is helping him?*
4. *Would you help this man if you could?*

WHAT DO YOU SEE?

What makes you think the man is blind? Do you see the cane he is holding? Point to it. What is he wearing that blind people often wear?

Please Pass the Rolls

Choosing to RESPECT OTHERS

What should this girl say? Don't you think she should say, "Please pass the rolls"? Her brother thinks so. He does not like for her to reach across the table that way. Mother does not like this either. Father will not like it as soon as he looks up. What the girl is doing is bad manners. People with bad manners do not show respect to other people around them. What would you like to say to this girl?

WHAT DO YOU SEE?
How many kinds of food do you see on the table? What would you think if each person reached across the table for each of these?

A TIME TO SHARE

1. *Do you like it when people show good manners?*
2. *Do you think people like you to show good manners?*
3. *How do good manners show respect to others?*

This Is the Way We Rake Leaves

Choosing to be HELPFUL

This is the way we rake leaves. If Father rakes them alone, it is a lot of work. If the boy rakes them alone, it is a lot of work for him. If the girl rakes them alone, it is a lot of work for her. But it isn't much work when the three work together. It's fun too! But don't you think it would be more fun if that other boy would help? Everyone would have less work to do. And the work would get done faster. What would you like to tell that boy on the chair?

WHAT DO YOU SEE?

Can you count the leaves? There are many more that you can't see. Father and the other two will rake them into big piles. They will have fun jumping into the leaves.

A TIME TO SHARE

1. *What is the boy on the chair doing?*
2. *What should he be doing?*
3. *Why do you think he would be happier if he helped Father and the others?*

Take That!

Choosing to CONTROL YOURSELF

This girl is surprised. You can see that. She and her brother have made a good tower. But something happened. A block didn't fit right. That made the boy angry. Look at his face, and you will see how angry he is. When people get angry they sometimes do silly things. They may even do things that hurt themselves or their friends. Do you see what this boy is doing? "Take that!" he shouts. Isn't it silly to knock down the whole tower because one block won't fit right? Isn't it silly for the boy to hurt his hand by smashing the blocks?

WHAT DO YOU SEE?

Look at the boy's face. How can you tell he is angry? What do his eyes tell you? What does his mouth tell you? Now look at the girl's face. How can you tell she is surprised?

A TIME TO SHARE

1. *What is the boy doing?*
2. *Why do you think this is silly?*
3. *What do you think his sister will say now?*

Please, God

Choosing to PRAY

1 Samuel 1:1-20

"Please, God, I want a baby." Poor Hannah! Do you see her there? She is praying that God will help her have a baby boy. Hannah has not had a baby. She is worried. What if she never has a baby? That would be terrible. Hannah does not know what to do. So she comes here to God's house. She asks God to help her. God will help her too! Do you see the priest behind Hannah? He hears her praying. Then he tells her that God will listen to her prayer. She will have a baby boy. And do you know what? Hannah did have a baby boy. He grew up to do God's work.

A TIME TO SHARE

1. *Why is Hannah praying?*
2. *What will the priest tell her?*
3. *What will God do for Hannah?*
4. *Why should we pray?*

WHAT DO YOU SEE?

What kind of clothing do you see on the priest? This was the special kind that only the most important priest could wear. This man was in charge of God's house. His name was Eli.

A Brave Boy

Choosing to have COURAGE

It's scary to stand up before a crowd. It's scary to do what this boy is doing. Mother is there. Father is there. Teacher is there. A lot of other people are there. Nobody will hurt the boy. But it is still scary. The boy needs lots of courage to do what he is doing. Do you think he has it?

WHAT DO YOU SEE?
Where do you think this is? Why do you think so? Are you afraid when you talk before a crowd like this?

A TIME TO SHARE

1. *What do you think the boy is doing?*
2. *Would you be afraid if you were the boy?*
3. *What would you do to become braver?*

I Love You, Little Puppy

Choosing to show LOVE

Look at that boy! He has found a new friend, hasn't he? That's the puppy he wants to take home. Mother asks, "Are you sure you wouldn't rather have this one?" What do you think the boy will say? No, he has found the puppy he wants to keep. Do you see what Father is doing already? He knows the boy has found his puppy. He is already paying for it. Don't you think that puppy is glad that someone loves it? Can't you hear the boy say, "I love you, little puppy"?

A TIME TO SHARE

1. *Why do you think the boy loves this puppy?*
2. *Why do you think the puppy is glad?*
3. *Do you have a pet? Do you love it?*
4. *Who are some others that you love?*

WHAT DO YOU SEE?

Why do you think this is a pet shop? What else do you see here besides the puppy and the family? Why do you think Father is buying that bag on the floor too?

I'm Sorry!

Choosing to be SORRY

What do you think has happened here? The boy is crying, isn't he? He is crying because the window is broken. Do you think he is crying because he thinks Father has broken it? If Father didn't do it, who did? Sometimes accidents happen. Something goes wrong and we really did not want it to happen. But it does! Then we are sorry when we see that someone gets hurt. Or something gets hurt. The boy did not want to knock his ball through the window. But he did. It was an accident. Now he is sorry. Father knows he is sorry. So he is forgiving the boy. He is also helping the boy feel better.

WHAT DO YOU SEE?

What got hurt here? Point to it. What makes you think a ball went through the window? Show two things that say it was a ball. Do you see the boy's cap? Do you see the bat?

A TIME TO SHARE

1. *Why is the boy crying?*
2. *How do you think the boy feels?*
3. *How do you know he is sorry?*
4. *Why does Father have his hand on the boy's shoulder? What is he saying to the boy?*

My Friend

Choosing to be FRIENDLY
1 Samuel 18:1-4

The young man sitting on the rock is David. He is a brave young man. He fought a giant and won. But David needs a good friend. We all need a good friend, don't we? Jonathan is a prince. He is the king's son. He wants to be David's best friend. Do you see what he is giving David? Those gifts show that Jonathan wants to be a best friend. Do you think David is glad to get these gifts? Do you think he is glad that Jonathan will be his best friend?

WHAT DO YOU SEE?
Jonathan is giving David some good gifts. Can you find his bow? His belt? His sword? Can you find Jonathan's robe?

A TIME TO SHARE

1. *Who is this young man on the rock?*
2. *Who is the man with the gifts?*
3. *Why is he giving these to David?*
4. *Why should friends help each other?*

This Is for You

Choosing to PUT OTHERS FIRST

I see two boys, don't you? They are both thirsty. But one of them grabs his cup and drinks every drop in it. He doesn't think about Mother. He doesn't think about Father. He thinks only of drinking that punch so he won't be thirsty. But do you see what the other boy is doing? Is he drinking the punch? Or is he doing something else with it? Why do you think this boy is doing something better than the other boy?

WHAT DO YOU SEE?
What do you see on the table? Point to the different kinds of food. What do you think is going on here? What else tells you that this is so?

A TIME TO SHARE

1. *What is the boy doing with his mother?*
2. *Why do you think he is doing this?*
3. *Why should we put others first?*
4. *How does this please Jesus?*

Someone Special

Choosing to show LOVE

Look at that boy and girl. Do you think they are happy? Someone special has come to see them. Can you guess who these special people are? That's right. They are Grandmother and Grandfather. The boy and girl are not sitting there quietly when these special people come through the door. They run and shout and tell Grandmother and Grandfather how much they love them. Don't you think these people all love each other?

WHAT DO YOU SEE?

Whose house is this? Do the boy and girl live here, or do Grandmother and Grandfather live here? Why do you think this? Which people have on their coats?

A TIME TO SHARE

1. *Why are the boy and girl so excited?*
2. *Which people here love each other?*
3. *Think of special people you love. How many can you name?*

WHAT DO YOU SEE?
What do you think the sign says? But what is the girl doing? What is the boy doing? Look at the boy's left hand. What does this mean?

Don't Pick the Flowers

Choosing to OBEY

"Don't pick the flowers." That's what the sign says. The boy knows what it says. He knows what he should not do. He knows what the girl should not do. Do you think the girl knows what the sign says? If she didn't know before, she does now! The boy is telling her, isn't he? Don't you think the girl should stop picking those flowers? Don't you think she should stop when she knows that it is wrong? What would you like to tell her about obeying?

A TIME TO SHARE

1. *Which one is obeying the sign?*
2. *What would you like to tell the boy?*
3. *What would you like to tell the girl?*
4. *Who is pleased when you obey?*

Follow the Leader

Choosing to FOLLOW

Have you ever heard a choir like this? Have you ever sung in one like this? If you have, you know that everyone must follow the choir leader. Then the choir will sound good. But what happens if a boy starts too late? What happens if a girl starts too early? The choir does not sound right, does it? That happens if the children do not follow the choir leader. Which kind of choir would you rather hear?

A TIME TO SHARE

1. *What are these people doing?*
2. *Which person is the choir leader?*
3. *Why should all the children follow her?*
4. *What happens if one does not?*

WHAT DO YOU SEE?

One of these children is not following the leader. Which one is it? Are the others following? What would you say to that boy if you were the choir leader?

Please Eat with Me

Choosing to be HELPFUL
2 Samuel 9

Do you see the king sitting on his throne? The king is David. He has lots of money. He has good food and a big house called a palace. But David wants to do something special. He wants to help someone. David once had a good friend named Jonathan. They were really best friends. Now Jonathan is dead. David wants to help someone in Jonathan's family. Then he finds out about this young man. His name is Mephibosheth. He is one of Jonathan's sons. David shares his home and food with him. He helps him get better clothes. David is a good friend, isn't he?

A TIME TO SHARE

1. *What does the king want to do?*
2. *Why does he want to be helpful?*
3. *How can you be helpful to your family?*
4. *How can you be helpful to your friends?*

WHAT DO YOU SEE?

Which man is Mephibosheth? He is crippled, isn't he? How do you know? Mephibosheth does not have much money. What do you think the king will do for him?

Half of My Sandwich

Choosing to SHARE

"Thank you!" That's what the girl is saying. She was going to make a sandwich after her brother had made his. But wasn't her brother kind? He did not eat the whole sandwich he made. Instead, he cut it in two and gave half to his sister. That's why his sister is saying, "Thank you!" She is pleased that her brother is sharing. Can you think of others who are pleased too?

A TIME TO SHARE

1. *What is the boy doing?*
2. *Why is his sister pleased?*
3. *What have you shared today?*

WHAT DO YOU SEE?

Where is the bread? Can you find the butter? What do you think is in the jar? What are the other things on the table?

Something to Smile About

Choosing to be HAPPY

It's time to go home. Sunday School was such fun today. You know that by the way the children are smiling. That's because they have something to smile about. Teacher helped them make some good pictures. Now they can show their good pictures to Mother and Father. Don't you think that will help Mother and Father smile too? Don't you think they are all happy that they came to Sunday School?

WHAT DO YOU SEE?
Why do you think this is Sunday School? Why isn't it the living room at home? Why isn't it the fire station?

A TIME TO SHARE

1. *What have the boy and girl just done?*
2. *Why do you think they look so happy?*
3. *What do you like to do in Sunday School?*
4. *Why are you glad to go to Sunday School?*

A Special Way to Give

Choosing to GIVE

Do you think those ducks are glad this girl came along? They are hungry. The girl knows this. She has something for the ducks to eat. But the ducks have nothing to give the girl. Do you think that makes the girl sad? It doesn't. She is just as happy to give them something to eat. She does not expect the ducks to give her anything. That's a special way to give, isn't it? Do you like to give when others can't give something back?

WHAT DO YOU SEE?
Where do you think this is? Why do you think so? How many ducks do you see? What do you think the girl is giving them?

A TIME TO SHARE

1. *What is the girl doing?*
2. *Why is she doing this?*
3. *What can the ducks give back to the girl?*
4. *Why is she still glad to give to them?*

God Can Do It!

Choosing to PRAY
1 Kings 18

Do you see Elijah? He is kneeling down. That's because he is praying. He is asking God to help him. Most of those people do not believe God can help them. They think a wicked god called Baal is the one who helps them. Elijah knows that Baal can't help. He is not even a real person. "Pray to Baal!" Elijah told these people. "Ask him to send fire." The people prayed. But how could Baal send fire? Now Elijah is praying to God. He is asking God to send fire on the altar. Do you see what is happening? Do you see what God is doing? God can do it, can't He?

WHAT DO YOU SEE?
Point to the big stone altar. What is that on top? Where did that fire come from?

A TIME TO SHARE

1. *What is Elijah doing?*
2. *What is he asking God to do?*
3. *Why do you think God can do this?*
4. *Why do you pray? What do you ask?*

Let Me Help You

Choosing to be KIND

Ouch! That girl on the sidewalk fell off her tricycle. That hurts. You know that if you have ever fallen on a concrete sidewalk. It hurts more if your friends laugh at you or make fun of you. But this friend is not laughing, is she? "Let me help you," she is saying to the girl who fell. Isn't that a kind thing to say? Isn't she a kind girl? Can you think of some friends who are kind like that?

A TIME TO SHARE

1. *What happened to the girl on the sidewalk?*
2. *Why does she need a kind friend now?*
3. *What do you think the kind friend is saying?*
4. *What would you say if you were there?*

WHAT DO YOU SEE?

What was the girl riding? How many wheels does it have? Can you count them? Where did the girl fall? What is it called? Do you think the girl hurts?

It's That Time Again

Choosing to be RESPONSIBLE

Do you know someone who owns a horse or pony? What do they have to do each day? Will the horse or pony feed itself? Will it give itself water or clean its own stall? Of course not. Then who will do it? This boy loves his pony. He has no one else to feed it. He has no one else to take care of it. So the boy is doing what he knows he should. It's that time again. He is doing this without being told. That is being responsible, isn't it?

A TIME TO SHARE

1. *Who told this boy to feed the pony?*
2. *Why is he doing this?*
3. *Do you like to be responsible?*
4. *Why does this please your parents?*

WHAT DO YOU SEE?

What kind of animal is this? Where is the pony? What do you see in this barn besides the pony?

There Goes My Balloon

Choosing to be SORRY

"Oh, no! There goes my balloon. I should have held onto the string better. Father, Father, can't you get it?" But Father can't get it. It is going up, up, up. It will go high into the sky. What can Father do? What can the girl do? What can Mother do? Now they can only watch the balloon go up into the sky. That's why the girl is sorry. She should have held the string tighter. But she didn't. Now she is sorry. What would you like to say to the girl?

A TIME TO SHARE

1. *What is happening to the balloon?*
2. *Why is it going up into the sky?*
3. *Why do you think the girl is sorry?*
4. *When were you sorry for something?*

WHAT DO YOU SEE?

Do you see the place where Father bought the balloon for the girl? Point to it. Point to three other things in this picture. Can you tell what each one is?

I Will Trust You

Choosing to TRUST

How would you like to be dressed up like that little dog? How would you like someone to push you around like that? The dog doesn't seem to mind. That's because he trusts the girl. He knows the girl will be careful. She will not push him too fast. She will be careful not to tip the doll buggy over. Do you think she will be careful?

A TIME TO SHARE

1. *What is the girl doing?*
2. *Does the dog seem afraid? Why not?*
3. *Do you think the girl will hurt the dog?*
4. *Who are some people you trust most?*

WHAT DO YOU SEE?

Can you point to a chimney, a doorknob, a lamp post, a fire hydrant, a wheel, a bonnet, a window, a shoe, and a roof?

Do You Like to be Good?

Choosing to be GOOD

Do you see the boy in the yard? He is not playing catch with his dog. He is chasing the poor dog with a stick. No wonder the dog is running away. But this boy sitting on the steps is not chasing his dog. He is telling his dog how much he loves him. He is saying some kind things to his dog. That's why the dog is listening. He likes to hear the boy say good things. He thinks this boy is a good boy. Do you?

A TIME TO SHARE

1. *Which boy is a good boy?*
2. *Why is he good? What is he doing?*
3. *Think of some ways you can be good.*
4. *Why does Jesus want you to be good?*

WHAT DO YOU SEE?

Can you find a garbage can? Point to a doorknob, a doormat, a stick, some steps, some gutters and a downspout, and some shoelaces.

I Want That

Choosing to be UNSELFISH
1 Kings 21

Now there is a selfish king. He has lots of money. He lives in a big palace. He has all that he needs. But he wants one more thing. He wants this poor man's vineyard. "I want that!" he tells the poor man. But this is a special vineyard. It belonged to the man's father and grandfather. He does not want to sell it. What do you think the selfish king will do now? When he tells the wicked queen about this man, the queen has the man killed. Then she tells the king to take the vineyard. What would you like to say to those bad people?

WHAT DO YOU SEE?
How do you know this is a vineyard? What do you see in the basket? What do you see growing? The tower in the back was a place where people stayed to guard the vineyard.

A TIME TO SHARE

1. *What does this selfish king want?*
2. *Why does the poor man want to keep it?*
3. *How does the selfish king get it?*
4. *What do you think God would say to this king?*

Shadow, Go Away

Choosing to have COURAGE

That girl is afraid, isn't she? You can almost hear her say, "Shadow, go away. You're too big and scary for me." Of course the shadow can't hurt the girl, can it? She knows that. When our rooms are dark, or an owl hoots, there is nothing really to be afraid of. But sometimes we are afraid anyway. What do you do when you are afraid? How do you find courage? This girl will pray. She will ask God to be with her. Then she will not need to be afraid. She will have Someone bigger than shadows with her to help her.

A TIME TO SHARE

1. *Why is the girl afraid?*
2. *What should she do?*
3. *What will you do next time you are afraid?*
4. *How can God give you courage?*

WHAT DO YOU SEE?

How could the girl make the shadow go away? Can the shadow do anything that the girl does not do? What would you like to tell the girl about her shadow?

I'll Get It!

Choosing to be HELPFUL

"Oh, no! There goes my new hat!" That poor girl doesn't know what to do. She is dressed up in her pretty dress. It is hard to chase a hat when you're dressed up like that. Perhaps she is going to Sunday School. Or she may be on her way to a birthday party. She needs someone to help her. She needs someone to chase her hat so she doesn't get messy. "I'll get it!" the boy says. Do you think he will?

WHAT DO YOU SEE?

Point to some things that show it is windy. You should find at least four things that are blowing.

A TIME TO SHARE

1. *Why can't the girl chase the hat easily?*
2. *What does the girl need?*
3. *How is the boy helping?*
4. *How have you helped someone this week?*

I Like That Story

Choosing to LISTEN

Do you like to hear mothers and fathers tell good stories? Do you like to hear grandpas and grandmas tell good stories? This boy is listening carefully to a grandpa tell a story. It is not his grandpa, but the man is a grandpa. He is a good storyteller too. Wouldn't you like to hear the story he is telling? What do you think it is about? The boy is a good listener. That helps this grandpa to be a good storyteller. It is no fun to tell a story if no one is listening.

WHAT DO YOU SEE?

Where do you think these two are? Point to five different things and tell what each one is.

A TIME TO SHARE

1. *What is this man doing?*
2. *What is the boy doing?*
3. *Why should we learn to listen to others?*
4. *Who should we listen to?*

A Time to Talk to God

Choosing to PRAY

This boy and girl are in church. You can see the big church window behind them, can't you? They could talk and whisper. They could play with some things they brought along. They could read some papers. But they aren't doing any of these things. What do you think they are doing? You are right. They are praying. They are talking to God. Do you like to do that when you go to church?

WHAT DO YOU SEE?
What kind of clothes are the boy and girl wearing? Why are their eyes closed? Do you see their hands? Do their hands look as if they are praying?

A TIME TO SHARE

1. *Who do you talk to when you pray?*
2. *What do you like to say to God?*
3. *Why do you think God listens to you?*
4. *What are some things God can do for you?*

It's Fun to Give

Choosing to GIVE
2 Kings 12:1-16

This good king had a good idea. He wanted to fix God's house. But he needed some extra money. "Please give money to fix God's house," he told his people. People then did not have coins. They did not have paper money. But they had chunks of gold and silver. So they brought their gold and silver. They put it in that big wooden chest. Before long there was enough money to fix God's house. Don't you think that good king had a good idea?

WHAT DO YOU SEE?
Do you see the big wooden chest? How is this different from the offering plate or basket in your church?

A TIME TO SHARE

1. *What are these people doing?*
2. *Do you think they want to fix God's house?*
3. *Is it fun to give for things like this?*
4. *Do you like to give money at your church?*

I Want to be First

Choosing to RESPECT OTHERS

It's time to get on the school bus. All of these boys and girls need to get on. But do you see that one boy? He wants to get on first. He pushes and shoves so that he can get there before the others. "I want to be first," he is saying. The other boys and girls do not like what he is doing. The bus driver does not like what he is doing. Do you like what he is doing? Why not?

WHAT DO YOU SEE?
Why do you think this is a school bus? How many children are trying to get on? Which boy wants to get on first?

A TIME TO SHARE

1. *What is that pushy boy trying to do?*
2. *Why does this not show respect to others?*
3. *What would you like to say to him?*
4. *Why does this not please Jesus?*

Thank You, Helper

Choosing to be HELPFUL

Father has been working hard at the office all day. He thought he would have to shovel snow when he came home. But look what a happy surprise he finds! His boy is working hard. He has shoveled almost all of the snow. Don't you think this makes Father happy? Don't you think it makes the boy happy too? He is happy that he could be helpful to Father. Aren't you happy when you can be helpful too?

A TIME TO SHARE

1. *Why do you think Father looks happy?*
2. *Why do you think the boy looks happy?*
3. *How have you been helpful today?*
4. *Why is Jesus pleased when you are helpful?*

WHAT DO YOU SEE?

Is this summer? Is it fall? Is it spring? How do you know? Is the boy shoveling the garden? What is he doing?

What Should I Do Now?

Choosing to FORGIVE

Oh, no! Look what that little girl is doing. What a mess! That may be her brother's favorite book too. You can see that her brother is not very happy about this. He would like to spank his little sister, but he won't. That's because the boy has been taught to forgive. He is glad when others forgive him for bad things. So he is glad to forgive his little sister for tearing up his good book. Since God forgives us for many big things, we should forgive others for some little things, shouldn't we?

A TIME TO SHARE

1. *What is the girl doing wrong?*
2. *What would the boy like to do?*
3. *What do you think the boy will do?*
4. *Why should you forgive others?*

WHAT DO YOU SEE?

What room of the house is this? Is it the kitchen? Why not? Is it the bathroom? Why not? What do you see that makes you think this is the boy's room?

Friend with a Smile

Choosing to be FRIENDLY

Here is a friend who comes almost every day. He brings birthday cards and letters from friends. He brings things for Mother and Father too. The postman could be grouchy, but he isn't. Do you see his smile? He is friendly. He likes to bring birthday cards and letters to boys and girls. He likes to talk with them. Do you think that is why they are friendly to him?

A TIME TO SHARE

1. *How do you know this man is friendly?*
2. *How do you know the children are friendly?*
3. *Name some adults who are friendly to you.*
4. *How does being friendly make us happier?*

WHAT DO YOU SEE?

What kind of work does this man do? How do you know? What is he carrying? How many things does he have for this family?

Don't Eat That!

Choosing to be HONEST

Mother is busy. The man at the store is busy. Nobody will see the boy eat that grape, will they? But Someone does see the boy. Do you know who that is? Do you think that Someone cares if the boy stole a grape? Do you think the man at the store cares? Do you think Mother cares? If all these people do not want the boy to steal, he shouldn't do it, should he?

WHAT DO YOU SEE?
Where is this? Point to some things that show that this is a store. Can you name some of the things you see in the picture?

A TIME TO SHARE

1. *Why isn't the boy being honest?*
2. *Who cares if he takes that grape?*
3. *Why does stealing hurt us?*
4. *Why do we feel better when we are honest?*

Let Me Take Care of You

Choosing to be LOYAL
Ruth 1:1-19

"What will I do?" Naomi wondered. She is the older lady. Naomi's husband died. But she has no money. And she is too old to go out in the fields to work. Naomi has no one to take care of her. "Let me take care of you," said Ruth. She loves Naomi. She wants to help her. Ruth will leave her home. She will go far away with Naomi. But do you see the other lady? She loves Naomi too. Her name is Orpah. She is not as loyal as Ruth. She will not go with Ruth and Naomi. That is why they are waving good-bye. Aren't you glad Ruth was loyal to Naomi? Now Naomi will have food to eat and a place to live.

A TIME TO SHARE

1. *Why is Naomi in trouble?*
2. *What will Ruth do for her?*
3. *How is Ruth being loyal?*
4. *Name some people who are loyal to you.*

WHAT DO YOU SEE?

How many women do you see? Which one is older? Which is Ruth? Which is Orpah? Which is Naomi?

Thank You for This Food

Choosing to PRAY

Why do all these people have their eyes closed? What are they doing? It's a party, with balloons and cake and ice cream. There's some punch to drink and candy and nuts in those little cups. Now it's time to eat. But first it is time to do something else. "Thank You for this food," Mother prays. She says this to Jesus. It's good to thank Jesus for our food each time we eat, isn't it?

WHAT DO YOU SEE?
Point to each thing that shows this is a party. How many balloons are there? How many pieces of cake? How old is the birthday boy or girl? How do you know?

A TIME TO SHARE

1. *What are these people doing?*
2. *Why should we thank Jesus for our food?*
3. *Do you thank Him before you eat?*
4. *Will you?*

Let's be Brave

Choosing to have COURAGE

Look out for that dog! He is barking as he runs toward the boy and girl. Do you think this boy and girl are afraid? Would you be afraid if you were one of them? "Let's be brave!" the boy tells the girl. That helps the girl have more courage. "We should pray!" the girl says. If they do, God will help them be brave. The dog will not bite them. He just wants to bark. But we all need a little extra courage at a time like this, don't we?

WHAT DO YOU SEE?
How many bicycle wheels do you see? Do you think those wheels will go faster now? Can you find a chimney? How many trees can you find in this picture?

A TIME TO SHARE

1. *Why are the boy and girl afraid?*
2. *What will they do to have more courage?*
3. *What do you do when you are afraid?*
4. *How can God help you have more courage?*

Don't Do That!

Choosing to be GOOD

There are two boys sitting behind that girl. One of them is trying to be good. The other is trying to be naughty. You can find the naughty one, can't you? Do you want to point to him? Do you want to tell him something? What do you think the other good boy will say? Do you know any boys who do naughty things like that? Do you know any boys who like to do good things instead?

A TIME TO SHARE

1. *What is that naughty boy doing?*
2. *Why is he not being good?*
3. *What should he be doing?*
4. *What are some good things you can do?*

WHAT DO YOU SEE?

Where do you think these children are? Why do you think so? Can you find two pencils? Can you find a chalkboard? Point to three pieces of paper.

A Man in a Tree

Choosing to be HONEST
Luke 19:1-10

Now there is something different. Not many men climb up into trees. But Zaccheus did. He wanted to see Jesus. He wanted to talk with Jesus. But Zaccheus could not even see Jesus. Zaccheus was too short and others in the crowd were too tall. That's why Zaccheus climbed up into the tree. There he could see Jesus. And Jesus saw him. "Zaccheus, come down," Jesus said. "I want to go to your house." Zaccheus was surprised. But he was glad. Now he could talk to Jesus. "I'm sorry for the way I have cheated people," Zaccheus said. Jesus forgave Zaccheus. And Zaccheus gave back the things he had stolen. Aren't you glad Zaccheus climbed that tree?

A TIME TO SHARE

1. *Why is Zaccheus in that tree?*
2. *Why is Zaccheus sorry?*
3. *What will he do now?*
4. *Why does Jesus want us to be honest?*

WHAT DO YOU SEE?

How many people do you see? What are they carrying? How is their clothing different from clothing your parents wear?

Father's Helper

Choosing to be HELPFUL

It's hard to hold a wreath and pound a nail at the same time. Father needs a helper. Do you see who that is? This boy is glad to help his father. He can hold the wreath. But he can't pound the nail. Do you know why? What would you like to tell this boy about being a good helper?

WHAT DO YOU SEE?
Which month of the year do you think this is? Why do you think this? Can you find the hammer? Can you find the nail?

A TIME TO SHARE

1. *What is Father doing?*
2. *Why does he need a helper?*
3. *Why do you think the boy is helping?*
4. *Why do helpers please Jesus?*

Please Come Here with Us

Choosing GOD'S WAY

Do you see the girl in front of the TV? She wants to keep on watching, doesn't she? But the family is ready to do something else. Do you know what it is? Father has the Bible open, ready to read. Mother and the boy are ready. But they must wait until the girl leaves the TV. Do you want to tell the girl to come? Don't you think that's what her brother is doing? It's time to choose Bible reading instead of TV, isn't it?

A TIME TO SHARE

1. *What is the family ready to do?*
2. *Why are three people waiting?*
3. *Why is it important to read the Bible together?*
4. *What can you do to help at Bible reading time?*

WHAT DO YOU SEE?

How many chairs can you count? How many have people in them? Who should sit in the empty chair?

Hurry! Grow!

Choosing to be PATIENT

It's springtime, time to plant seeds. Do you see the garden? This boy and girl dug the soil and hoed it until it was soft. Then they planted seeds and put water on them. But look what they are doing. They are waiting for the seeds to grow. Do you think they should do that? What would you like to say to them?

A TIME TO SHARE

1. *What did this boy and girl do?*
2. *Why are they sitting there?*
3. *What should they do while they wait for the seeds to grow?*

WHAT DO YOU SEE?

How many seed packages do you see? What kind of seeds were in each packet? What else do you see?

Stop That, Cat!

Choosing to FORGIVE

Oh, oh! Where is the goldfish? It was in the bowl. But it is not there now, is it? Where do you think it is? The boy and girl know. They see the cat sitting there by the bowl. They see the cat lick its mouth. You know what that means, don't you? That naughty cat had dinner, but it was not cat food. Do you think the boy and girl will be angry at the cat? Do you think they will forgive the cat? Would you?

A TIME TO SHARE

1. *What happened here?*
2. *What do the boy and girl see?*
3. *What do you think they will say?*
4. *Why should we forgive others when they do wrong?*

WHAT DO YOU SEE?

How do you know that is a fishbowl? Why do you think the cat ate the goldfish? What is the cat wearing? Why is the bell on the cat's neck?

Listen! Jesus Is Talking!

Choosing to LISTEN
John 3

Listen! Jesus is talking. Would you like to know what He is saying to that man? He is telling that man how God helps us know Him. He is telling Nicodemus how to get to heaven. You would listen to Jesus tell you that, wouldn't you? Nicodemus did. He listened to every word that Jesus said. You can still listen to the words that Jesus said. They are in your Bible. Jesus can tell you exactly the same thing He told Nicodemus. Listen! Jesus is talking.

WHAT DO YOU SEE?
How do you know that the wind is blowing here? Jesus talked about the wind. He told Nicodemus that God moves as quietly and as secretly as the wind.

A TIME TO SHARE

1. *What did Jesus tell Nicodemus?*
2. *Why is that important?*
3. *Do you know how to get to heaven? Jesus tells us. It is in your Bible.*

What Will Kitty Do?

Choosing to be KIND

Do you see the happy kitty? She is purring. That's because the girl is so kind to her. The girl is petting the kitty. She is saying nice things to her. That's why the kitty is so happy. But look! Someone else is not going to be kind to the kitty. What is that naughty boy going to do? Do you think the kitty will be happy when he does that? What will the poor kitty do?

A TIME TO SHARE

1. *What is that naughty boy doing?*
2. *Why is that not kind?*
3. *What would you say to that boy?*
4. *Can you name three kind people you know?*

WHAT DO YOU SEE?

Do you see the kitty's face? Is it sad or happy? What would you say about the girl's face? What would you say about the boy's face?

Sand Castles Are Fun

Choosing to be FRIENDLY

What is better than a day at the beach? It's fun to make sand castles. It's even more fun to make them with someone else. This boy and girl think so. They want to be friends with the other children. Do you see that? They are asking the other children to play with them. What kind of sand castle do you think the five of them will make? It will be a sand castle made by five friends, won't it?

WHAT DO YOU SEE?

How many boys do you see? How many girls do you see? What do you see that the boys and girls have made?

A TIME TO SHARE

1. *Why is it more fun to play with someone instead of playing alone?*
2. *Do you like to be friendly? Why?*
3. *Name some people who are very friendly.*
4. *What do you especially like about them?*

Take Off Those Boots

Choosing to RESPECT OTHERS

It's time to go inside. The boy and girl have been playing out in the slushy snow. Their boots are messy. Do you think they should walk into the house with their boots on? What should they do first? This boy and girl are taking off their boots. That is a good way to do it, isn't it? That shows Mother that they respect her and the house. It would be rude to walk into the house with messy boots, wouldn't it?

WHAT DO YOU SEE?

How do you know that the boy and girl are outside? Point to some things that show they are not inside the house.

A TIME TO SHARE

1. *Why are the boy and girl taking off their boots? Why not wear them inside?*
2. *How do you show respect to your parents?*
3. *How do you show respect to God?*

Stop! Think! Don't Say It!

Choosing to CONTROL YOURSELF

Ouch! That hurts when you fall down. But it hurts more when your friends laugh at you. They don't want to be unkind. But friends sometimes like to laugh at a time like this, don't they? This girl is not happy about falling. She is not happy about her friends laughing at her. You can see that by her face. But she is trying to control herself. She is trying not to say something angrily to her friends. Don't you think she is doing the right thing?

WHAT DO YOU SEE?

What time of year is this? How do you know? Can you point to some ice? Can you find some snow? Can you point to some winter trees? What kind of clothes are the children wearing?

A TIME TO SHARE

1. *When were you angry last?*
2. *Why did you get angry?*
3. *Did you say something you shouldn't?*
4. *Why does God want us to control ourselves?*

Little Chick, I Love You

Choosing to show LOVE

"Little chick, I love you." Can't you hear this girl say something like this? The little chick hears. It does not understand the words. But somehow it knows that the girl loves it. Perhaps it is the way the girl talks. Or is it the way she holds the chick in her hands? Or does the chick feel something without the words? No one knows for sure. But you can see that the chick is not trying to get away. Perhaps it would like to say, "I love you too."

A TIME TO SHARE

1. *Why do you think the girl loves the chick?*
2. *Why do you think the chick knows that?*
3. *Does your dog or cat know you love it?*
4. *How do you think it knows?*

WHAT DO YOU SEE?

Where does this girl live? Does she live in a big city? Does she live on a farm? How do you know?

Walls Are Not Built in a Day

Choosing to be PATIENT
Nehemiah 2:17—7:3

Look at those men working. They have a big job ahead of them. Do you see some of them pulling that big stone up the hill? That is only one stone. They must pull many stones like that. They must lift them up and put them in the right place on the wall. How would you like to do that all day? Nehemiah and his workers did it. While they worked some bad men tried to stop them. Don't you think Nehemiah and his men wished that the wall was done? Of course they did. But they could only put one stone in place, and then another. They had to be patient. Walls are not built in a day. Many other things are not done in a day. Many other things are not done in a day either. Have you learned to be patient?

A TIME TO SHARE

1. *What are Nehemiah and his men doing?*
2. *Why can't they do this in one day?*
3. *How does this teach patience?*
4. *Are you being patient about something?*

WHAT DO YOU SEE?

How do you know these men are building a wall? Point to some things that tell you. Can you name these things?

Won't You Come In?

Choosing to PUT OTHERS FIRST

Now there is a gentleman. Do you see what the boy is doing? The boy is going outside to play. He could have run through the door first. But Mother came with her arms filled with packages. What would you do? This boy decided to put Mother first. That's why he is holding the door open so Mother can come through first. What would you like to say to the boy?

A TIME TO SHARE

1. *What is the boy doing?*
2. *Why didn't he run through the doorway first instead of letting Mother come in first?*
3. *Why should we put others first?*

WHAT DO YOU SEE?

Is the boy on the inside or outside of the house? Is Mother coming into the house or going out of it? Where do you think Mother has been? How do you know?

Oh! Oh!

Choosing to be SORRY

We all make mistakes, don't we? This boy just made a big mistake. Look at that mess on the floor. Kitty wants to play in it. But the boy doesn't like what happened. He is sorry that he dropped the juice. Mother knows it was an accident. She knows the boy is sorry because he says he is. Can't you hear him say, "I'm sorry, Mother"? Do you think Mother will forgive him? Of course she will. Wouldn't you? But guess who gets to clean up the mess?

WHAT DO YOU SEE?
What room is this? Is it the living room? Is it the bathroom? Is it the kitchen?

A TIME TO SHARE

1. *What mistake did the boy make?*
2. *What do you think he is saying?*
3. *Why do you think Mother will forgive him?*
4. *Why should you forgive others?*

Pumpkin Time

Choosing to be THANKFUL

Have you ever gone to a farm stand to buy pumpkins or Indian corn? This family is looking for a good pumpkin for a jack-o'-lantern. While they are there, they will buy some Indian corn and perhaps some squash. It's a good time to be thankful for God's good things, isn't it? Can you think of some good things that God has given you? Would you like to thank Him for them?

WHAT DO YOU SEE?

What time of year is this? How do you know? Can you name some of the things you could buy at this farm stand? What do you see in the sky? How does this tell you it is fall?

A TIME TO SHARE

1. *Why should this boy and girl be thankful?*
2. *Why do you think they are thankful?*
3. *Why should you be thankful?*
4. *Who will you thank today?*

Let Me Serve You

Choosing to be RESPONSIBLE
Luke 15:11-24

Do you see how this father is hugging his boy? Would you like to know why? One day the son wanted all of the money his father would give him. He ran away from home. Then he spent the money. He had nothing left. That young man got hungry. But no one would help him. He had to earn some money by feeding pigs. Then he remembered his wonderful home. He remembered his kind father. The young man came home. He told his father, "I'm sorry. Let me serve you." Do you see how the father is welcoming him home? That's the way God welcomes us when we tell Him, "I'm sorry. Let me serve You." Have you done that?

WHAT DO YOU SEE?
How do you know this is the father's home? How do you know the son and father are happy?

A TIME TO SHARE

1. *Why is this young man happy now?*
2. *Why is his father happy?*
3. *How did the young man learn to be more responsible?*

I'm Glad You're There

Choosing to be LOYAL

This girl looks happy, doesn't she? Do you know why? You can see that she is snuggled down in her soft, warm bed. But that is not the real reason she is happy. She is happy because Mother and Father are there to say good night. They do this every night. They were there last night. The girl knows they will be there to say good night tomorrow night too. Mother and Father are loyal to their girl. They are there when she needs them. But the girl is loyal to them too. She loves her parents. She will not do anything to hurt them. That's why they are happy!

A TIME TO SHARE

1. *Who is there with the girl?*
2. *When do they say good night to her?*
3. *Why does this make the girl happy?*
4. *Why should we be loyal to each other?*

WHAT DO YOU SEE?

Is this the kitchen? Is it the bathroom? Is it the living room? Why do you think this is the girl's room?

What Do You Hear?

Choosing to TRUST

Do you see what this doctor is doing? That thing is called a stethoscope. The doctor can listen to your heartbeat with that. Don't you think the boy wants to ask, "What do you hear?" Perhaps the doctor will tell him. But the boy must trust the doctor to do what is best. The boy does not know how to check his heart. He does not know how to give himself a shot or take his blood pressure. But the doctor does. Aren't you glad you can trust your doctor?

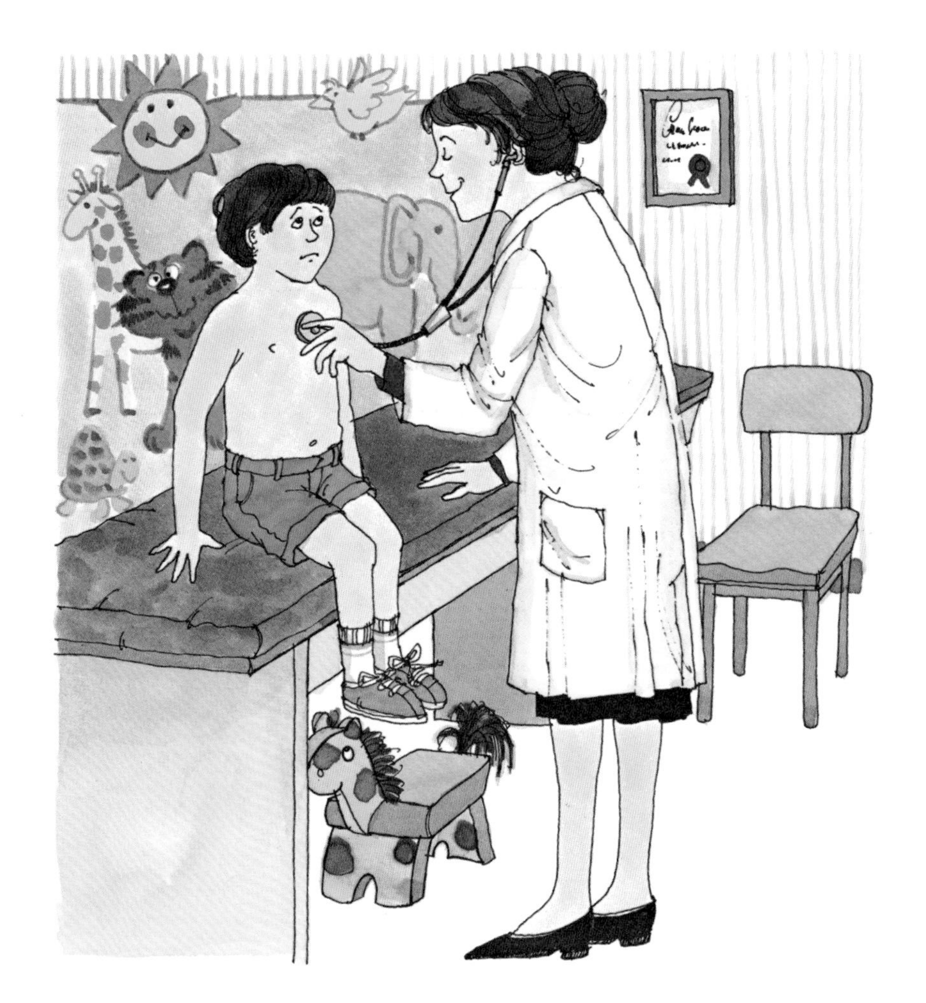

A TIME TO SHARE

1. *Why is the boy here?*
2. *Why does the boy need the doctor?*
3. *Why should he trust the doctor?*
4. *Why should you trust God to help you?*

WHAT DO YOU SEE?

How do you know this is a doctor's office? What are some things that a doctor does? How can a doctor help you?

Together

Choosing GOD'S WAY

Here's a family that likes to be together. Do you see how much they are enjoying an evening by the fire? The girl is playing with her puppy. The boy is playing with the kitten. And do you see Mother and Father? They are having fun watching, and being together. These family members could choose to argue and fight. They could choose to do things in different parts of the house. But they think being together is God's way. That's why they choose to be together.

A TIME TO SHARE

1. *Why do you think this family likes to be together?*
2. *How does this please God?*
3. *Why do you like to be with your family?*

WHAT DO YOU SEE?

Do you think this is summer or winter? Find two things that tell you.

Jesus Loves You

Choosing to show LOVE
Mark 10:13-16

Everyone in town wants to see Jesus. But look who gets to talk with Him! He is not talking to the most important man or woman. He is talking to some children. That's because Jesus loves children. He wants them to know that. Do you think they do? Do you know that Jesus loves you?

WHAT DO YOU SEE?
Do the children seem afraid of Jesus? Why don't they? Why do they look so happy to be with Him?

A TIME TO SHARE

1. *Why do you think Jesus loves children?*
2. *Why should you love Jesus?*
3. *Do you like to talk with Jesus?*
4. *Will you tell Him that you love Him?*

Come Here! Come Here!

Choosing to be HAPPY

Look at that big mushroom! Have you ever seen such a big one? This father has never seen such a big mushroom. "Come here! Come here!" he says. Look at the rest of the family running. They know that Father has found something exciting. Don't you think this is a happy family? They are happy doing things together. That's a good way to be happy, isn't it?

WHAT DO YOU SEE?
Where do you think this family is hiking—in a city alley, inside a school building, or in a woods? Why do you think this? Point to some things you find in a woods.

A TIME TO SHARE

1. *Why is this family happy?*
2. *What are they doing together?*
3. *Why are you happy when you are with your family? What things do you do?*

A Ride on the Merry-go-round

Choosing to be HONEST

Do you like to ride on a merry-go-round? This boy and girl do. They are buying tickets, and will soon be riding on the merry-go-round back there. But look at that other boy. He is not buying a ticket, is he? He is trying to get in without one. That boy is not honest, is he? He is cheating. Do you think he will have fun on the merry-go-round? It isn't fun to cheat, is it? The boy and girl who are honest will have more fun.

WHAT DO YOU SEE?
How many children can you find in this picture? Can you find six? How many balloons can you find?

A TIME TO SHARE

1. *What are these children going to do?*
2. *Which children are honest?*
3. *Which boy is cheating?*
4. *Who will be happier? Why?*

Come with Me

Choosing to be KIND

Here is a kind big brother. It's no fun to go out alone to trick-or-treat. It could be scary too. "Come with me," the girl's big brother says. You can see how much the girl wants to go with her big brother. She thinks he is kind to let her do this. Mother thinks he is kind to do this too. What do you think?

A TIME TO SHARE

1. *Where are the girl and boy going?*
2. *How is the boy being kind?*
3. *Why does this please Mother?*
4. *Why does this please Jesus?*

WHAT DO YOU SEE?

What month of the year is this? How do you know? What kind of costume is the girl wearing? What kind of costume is the boy wearing? What did you wear last time?

May I Help You?

Choosing to be HELPFUL

"May I help you?" the kind lady asks. This girl is glad to hear what the lady says. She is buying a gift for Mother. But she needs help. The lady knows more about these things than the girl does. So the girl listens carefully. She trusts the lady. She is glad the lady is so helpful. What do you think the girl will buy for Mother?

A TIME TO SHARE

1. *What is the girl doing?*
2. *Why does she need help?*
3. *What is the kind lady doing?*
4. *Who have you helped this week? How?*

WHAT DO YOU SEE?

What kind of store is this? Is it a grocery store? Is it a drugstore? Is it a bookstore? How do you know what it is?

Sit!

Choosing to OBEY

"Sit!" That's what the boy is saying to his dog. The dog is learning to obey. Do you see how the dog is sitting? He likes to obey. The boy is pleased that the dog obeys. You can see that the girl is pleased too. Don't you think they should be? God is pleased when you obey. So are your parents. Don't you think they should be? You should be pleased too.

A TIME TO SHARE

1. *What is the dog doing?*
2. *Why does this please the boy?*
3. *Who is pleased when you obey?*
4. *Why should you obey?*

WHAT DO YOU SEE?

The boy has two hands. What are his two hands doing? The girl has two hands. What are her two hands doing?

I Forgive You

Choosing to FORGIVE

Genesis 45:1-15

Those men with beards did something terrible. Long ago, they sold their brother Joseph as a slave. They thought he would die, but he didn't. He became governor over the land of Egypt. That's Joseph with the strange-looking belt and head covering. Joseph has been selling grain to his brothers. But they did not know he is Joseph. He did not want to tell them yet. He wanted to be sure they were sorry that they had sold him. Now he knows they are sorry, so he tells them who he is. "I forgive you," Joseph tells them. That's why they all look happy. That should make people happy, shouldn't it?

WHAT DO YOU SEE?

Which man is Joseph? He is dressed like that because he lives in Egypt. Benjamin is the youngest brother. Can you point to him? Joseph likes Benjamin more than his other brothers. You can see that, can't you?

A TIME TO SHARE

1. *Why are these people happy?*
2. *Which brother is forgiving the others?*
3. *Would you like to forgive someone?*
4. *Would you like someone to forgive you?*

A Good Story

Choosing to LISTEN

Do you see what Mother is doing? She is reading a good story. The boy is listening carefully. He wants to hear every word Mother reads. So does the girl. They could be thinking about other things, but they aren't. They could be running around, trying to do something else while Mother reads, but they aren't. They are listening. Don't you think they should?

WHAT DO YOU SEE?
Why do you think this is almost bedtime? Why isn't it the middle of the day? Point to some things that tell you it is almost bedtime.

A TIME TO SHARE

1. *Who is reading?*
2. *Who is listening?*
3. *Why should you listen to Mother and Father?*
4. *Why should you listen to God's Word?*

What a Story!

Choosing to tell the TRUTH

Oh! Oh! What a story that boy is telling. It just isn't true. He knows it isn't true. The younger boy knows it isn't true. And Mother and Father know it isn't true. Jesus knows it isn't true too because He can hear what the boy is saying. That boy should tell the truth. Don't you think so? What would you like to say to him?

WHAT DO YOU SEE?
Look at each person's face. What do you see? What do you think each person is thinking?

A TIME TO SHARE

1. *Which boy is not telling the truth?*
2. *Who knows that he is lying?*
3. *Why should you tell the truth?*
4. *Who wants you to tell the truth?*

Stop That!

Choosing to be HONEST

That poor little dog is trying to eat his dinner. But how can he with that big dog growling at him? That big dog is a bully. He wants to steal the little dog's dinner. What would you think if a big bully stole your dinner from you? That would be wrong, wouldn't it? But here comes someone to help. "Stop that!" he shouts. He will make that big dog go away. The big dog wants to steal. He doesn't want to be honest. But he must stop stealing and be honest when someone bigger makes him do it. Don't you wish the big dog would not want to steal his friend's dinner?

A TIME TO SHARE

1. *How is the big dog stealing?*
2. *Does he want to be honest?*
3. *Why should you want to be honest?*
4. *Who wants you to be honest?*

WHAT DO YOU SEE?

Which dog should be eating that dinner? Which one should not be eating it? Who will stop the big dog from stealing?

Whooo

Choosing to PRAY

Whooo. That's what the owl says. The owl won't hurt anyone. This boy knows that. But it is still scary to be out at night and hear *whooo.* Are you ever afraid at night? What do you do? This boy is choosing to pray. When he does, he will not be afraid. He will remember that God is with him, even at night. That's good to remember, isn't it?

A TIME TO SHARE

1. *Why is the boy afraid?*
2. *What will he do?*
3. *How will that help him not be afraid?*
4. *How can God help you not be afraid?*

WHAT DO YOU SEE?

Can you find: a house, an owl, some leaves, a stump, the boy, a tree?

May I Water Your Camels?

Choosing to be KIND

Genesis 24

That man with the camel has come on a long trip. He is looking for a wife for Isaac, a young man back home. That's the way some people got married then. "Lord, show me the right girl," the man prayed. "Let the right girl ask to water my camels." Before long, this beautiful girl came to the well where the man had prayed. "May I water your camels?" she asked. The man was so happy. He knew now that this kind girl was the right one for Isaac. She was the one God had chosen. "Thank You, Lord," he prayed.

A TIME TO SHARE

1. *What is this girl doing?*
2. *How do you know she is kind?*
3. *How can you be kind to others?*
4. *When you are kind, whom do you please?*

WHAT DO YOU SEE?

That round stone wall is the top of a well. The girl got water by dropping the waterpot into the well and pulling it out with a rope. How do you get your water?

Something to Make You Happy

Choosing to be HAPPY

Who doesn't like a beautiful balloon? This girl likes them. She wants to take one home. But which one? Will it be the red balloon or the yellow one? Will it be the blue balloon or the green one? The girl will choose one. It will be fun to carry it home. The girl will be happy to have the balloon. But she will be happiest because Father bought it for her. Gifts from Father or Mother are special, aren't they?

A TIME TO SHARE

1. *What is the girl doing?*
2. *Who is giving the girl the balloon?*
3. *Why does this make her happy?*
4. *Has something made you happy lately?*

WHAT DO YOU SEE?

How many balloons do you see? How many will the girl need to take home to make her happy? Who else do you see in the picture besides the girl?

What Do You See?

Choosing to GIVE

Look! What do you see? It's time to eat and this mother bird has dinner ready. You wouldn't want your mother to feed you a big worm for dinner, would you? That's because you are not a bird. These little birds think a worm is the best dinner of all. Do you see their mouths open? They are glad their mother is giving them something good to eat. Are you glad when your mother gives you good food to eat? Do you thank her for the good food?

A TIME TO SHARE

1. *Who is giving something here?*
2. *What do you think Mother is saying?*
3. *What do you think the girl is saying?*
4. *What do you say when you get a gift?*

WHAT DO YOU SEE?

What is Mother doing? Can you find the clothes basket? Point to the clothespins. How many can you find?

Doing What I Should

Choosing to be RESPONSIBLE

You like to brush your teeth each morning, don't you? This boy does. When he doesn't, he thinks his teeth feel like they have fur on them. He doesn't like his teeth to feel that way. So he brushes his teeth as soon as he gets up. Mother does not have to tell him. Father does not have to tell him. He does it without being told. That's being responsible, isn't it?

WHAT DO YOU SEE?
How many things can you find that are in your bathroom? Can you find the toothpaste? Where is the toothbrush? How many towels do you see?

A TIME TO SHARE

1. *Why does the boy brush his teeth?*
2. *Who has to tell him to do it?*
3. *How are you responsible? What do you do without being told?*

Happy Home

Choosing to show LOVE

Here is a happy home. Do you see Mother and Father? Are they quarreling? Are they angry with each other? Are they shouting at each other? Mother and Father love each other. They are not ashamed to say, "I love you." Mother is happy when Father says that. Father is happy when Mother says that. Their children are happy too. It makes them feel warm and good when they know Mother and Father love each other. Love keeps people from shouting at each other. Love keeps us saying "I love you" to each other. No wonder everyone is smiling.

A TIME TO SHARE

1. *How do you know Mother and Father love each other?*
2. *Why does this make the children happy?*
3. *How can you help to make your family happy?*

WHAT DO YOU SEE?

Do you think the dog and cat are contented? Do they have anything to fear in this house? Does anyone have anything to fear?

See the Happy King

Choosing to be HAPPY

2 Samuel 6

Look at that happy man with the harp! He is King David. Do you know why he is happy? He is bringing a beautiful chest into the city where he lives. It is a special golden chest. Many years before, God told people how to make it. For a long time it was in a special place in God's tent-house. But some people stole God's golden chest. It has not been in God's tent-house for many years. But King David knows God's golden chest should be in God's tent-house. He is bringing it there. Now you know why he is so happy. Now you know why all the people are smiling and singing.

WHAT DO YOU SEE?

The golden chest is covered with a cloth. Can you find it? What are some people doing? Why are the children happy?

A TIME TO SHARE

1. *What are these people doing?*
2. *Why are they so happy?*
3. *Why do you think this pleases God?*
4. *What can you do today to please God?*

Thank You, Mother

Choosing to be THANKFUL

What are some things you cannot do? How many of these does Mother do? How many does Father do? How many does someone else do? Here is a girl who cannot sew a button on her coat. But Mother can. And Mother is sewing a button on the girl's coat. Don't you think this girl is thankful that Mother is doing this for her? You would be, wouldn't you? And you are thankful for all the good things Father does for you too, aren't you?

WHAT DO YOU SEE?

Point to some things that tell you Mother is sewing. Can you find the needle? Do you see the thread? Where is the sewing basket?

A TIME TO SHARE

1. *Why isn't the girl sewing her button on?*
2. *Why is Mother doing it?*
3. *Name some things Mother and Father do for you that you can't do. Do you thank them?*

I'm Glad to Meet You

Choosing to RESPECT OTHERS

What are these people doing? We can figure it out, can't we? The man with the glasses is Father. He is introducing his son to his friend. Father's friend is glad to meet this boy. He wants to shake hands with the boy, just as he would do with the bank president. And do you see what the boy is doing? He is going to shake this man's hand, just like a grown-up. The man is showing respect to the boy, treating him like a man. The boy is showing respect to the man, treating him like a friend. Don't you think Father is proud of his boy? Don't you think Father is proud of his friend?

WHAT DO YOU SEE?
Are these people on their way to church? Why don't you think so? What do you think they are planning to do?

A TIME TO SHARE
1. *How is the boy showing respect?*
2. *How is Father's friend showing respect?*
3. *Father is showing respect too. How?*
4. *How can you show respect to parents?*

Helping Is Fun

Choosing to be HELPFUL

It's that scary time of year again. Do you see what Father is doing? This boy and girl see. They want to help Father. That's why the girl got the candle ready. The boy tells Father the kind of face to carve. Father is a helper too, isn't he? He is helping his boy and girl have fun.

A TIME TO SHARE

1. *How is Father helping the boy and girl?*
2. *How is the girl helping?*
3. *How is the boy helping?*
4. *Why is helping fun?*

WHAT DO YOU SEE?

Can you find the dog? Can you find the cat? Point to the candle the girl is holding. Point to the lid of the pumpkin.

Come Out and be a Friend

Choosing to have COURAGE

I see two dogs, don't you? One is bigger. He looks more fierce. If you were the little dog wouldn't you be afraid of that big, mean-looking dog? The little dog is afraid. That's easy to see. He thinks the big dog might hurt him. He wants to stay in his house where he will be safe. Actually the big dog isn't mean. He just looks that way. He will not hurt the little dog. He wants to be a friend. The boys know that. So they are trying to get the little dog to come out. Do you think he will?

WHAT DO YOU SEE?
How many dogs do you see? How many boys do you see? How many of them will soon be friends?

A TIME TO SHARE

1. *Why is the little dog afraid?*
2. *Does the big dog want to be a friend?*
3. *Should the little dog be afraid?*
4. *Are you afraid of something? What?*

Yes, I Will Build a Boat

Choosing to OBEY

Genesis 6—9

That man holding the wood is Noah. He loves God and wants to do things to please God. One day God talked to Noah. "Build a big boat here," God told him. Noah was surprised. There was no big lake or river. There was no ocean. Where would the boat go? Then God told Noah, "I will send a big flood. There will be water everywhere. The boat will keep you safe." Noah listened to God. He did all that God told him to do. So God kept Noah safe when the flood came. Do you think Noah was glad then that he obeyed God?

A TIME TO SHARE

1. *What did God tell Noah to do?*
2. *Why did Noah do it?*
3. *Why should we obey God?*
4. *Why should you obey parents?*

WHAT DO YOU SEE?

Do you know what that big thing is behind Noah? It is the ark, the big boat Noah built. Point to some things that show that Noah is not done yet.

Thank You for Someone Special

Choosing to be THANKFUL

Here is someone special! Do you see the new baby? Father sees her through the nursery window. Brother and sister see her too. They are so happy that God gave them their new sister. They can't hold her yet, but they will when she comes home from the hospital with Mother. They are thankful for the new baby sister. They know what fun they will have with her at home. Tonight when they pray they will thank God for someone special.

A TIME TO SHARE

1. *Why are the boy and girl so happy?*
2. *What will they do when the baby comes home?*
3. *Why do you think they are thankful?*
4. *Who do you thank when you are thankful?*

WHAT DO YOU SEE?

How do you know this is a hospital? Who is holding the baby? Why can't the boy and girl go inside and hold the baby?

Should You Do That

Choosing to be GOOD

Wouldn't you like to say something to that boy on the fence? The other boy would. He is saying something too. What do you think he is telling the other boy? Do you think he is scolding him? Do you think he might be saying, "Don't do that"? He should. That boy is not being good, is he? We should never bother birds when they are trying to hatch their eggs. If you were the boy on the ground, what would you say to that boy who is bothering the bird?

A TIME TO SHARE

1. *What is the naughty boy trying to do?*
2. *Why should he not do this?*
3. *What should the other boy tell him?*
4. *Why should we try to be good?*

WHAT DO YOU SEE?

Do you see the bird? How many eggs do you see in the nest? Find a rock. Find a fence. What else do you see in the picture?

Lord, I Am Listening

Choosing to RESPECT OTHERS

Exodus 3

That man is Moses. He came here with some sheep. Moses thought he was alone here. But he wasn't. Someone spoke to him from this burning bush. Do you know who that was? Moses knows. It is God who is speaking. Moses listens carefully. Do you see that he is kneeling down on his knees? That is Moses' way to show honor or respect to God. Do you sometimes kneel down like that to pray? Many people do. They want God to know that they honor Him and respect Him.

WHAT DO YOU SEE?

Do you see that the bush is burning? It keeps on burning, but never burns up. God did that so Moses would know that something special was happening. He would know that God is there.

A TIME TO SHARE

1. *Why is Moses down on his knees?*
2. *Why should people honor or respect God?*
3. *What do you do when you pray?*
4. *How else can you honor or respect God?*

Stop! Go!

Choosing to OBEY

When that light turns red, what should you do? What should you do when it turns green? This boy knows that. That's why he has stopped. He knows that a red light says "Stop!" If he doesn't stop, he may hurt someone. Or he may get hurt. Who wants to get hurt or who wants to hurt someone? The boy doesn't. He knows it is better to obey that traffic light. He's a wise boy, isn't he?

WHAT DO YOU SEE?
What kind of light is that? Do you know the three colors on a traffic light? What does green tell you to do? What does red tell you to do? Yellow says, "The light is changing color. Get ready!"

A TIME TO SHARE

1. *Why has the boy stopped?*
2. *Why does he want to obey the light?*
3. *Whom should you obey? Why?*
4. *What happens if you do not obey?*

Thin Ice

Choosing to be RESPONSIBLE

"Stop! Can't you read that sign?" It says "thin ice," doesn't it? That boy is headed for trouble. If he gets too close to the thin ice, he may fall in the water. The girl knows that. She is shouting at the boy to get back. That foolish boy is not being responsible, is he? Wouldn't you like to say something to that boy? What would you tell him?

WHAT DO YOU SEE?
How do you know this is thin ice? The sign says so, but two other things tell you. Can you find the hole? Can you find the cracks in the ice?

A TIME TO SHARE

1. *What is the boy doing that he shouldn't do?*
2. *Why shouldn't he skate here?*
3. *Why is it foolish to do something we know is wrong? Who can get hurt?*

The New Baby

Choosing to be THANKFUL

Oh, oh, oh! What a special time this is. Mother and Father are just coming home from the hospital. They have their new baby. Do you see how happy this girl is? She is now a sister. She is now a BIG sister. No wonder the girl is so happy. She claps her hands and says, "Oh, oh, oh!" Wouldn't you do this too if you had a new baby in your house? Wouldn't you be thankful, just as this girl is?

A TIME TO SHARE

1. *Why is this girl so happy?*
2. *Who is the new family member?*
3. *Now what can the girl call herself?*
4. *Why should you be thankful for good things?*

WHAT DO YOU SEE?

What makes you think Mother and Father are just coming home from the hospital? Point to three things that show this.

My Gift for You

Choosing to show LOVE
John 12:1-8

Look! Mary is pouring expensive perfume on Jesus' feet. One man does not like that. He thinks she is wasting money. But Mary does not think that. She wants to do something special for Jesus. He has done some very special things for her. This is her way to show love to Jesus. Do you think her gift is too good for Jesus?

A TIME TO SHARE

1. *What is Mary doing?*
2. *Why is she doing this?*
3. *How does this show love to Jesus?*
4. *How can you show love to Jesus?*

WHAT DO YOU SEE?

What kind of bottle does Mary have? It is made of stone. The perfume is oily, but smells good.

Please Sit Down

Choosing to RESPECT OTHERS

That poor woman is tired. She has been shopping all afternoon. Now her arms are filled with packages. No wonder she is sad when she gets on the bus. There is no place to sit down. Don't you think the woman is sad? When you're tired and your arms are filled with things, you want to sit down too, don't you? But look! There is a boy who sees the tired woman. "Please sit down," he tells her. The boy stands up so the woman can sit where he was sitting. That's a good way to show respect for the lady, isn't it?

A TIME TO SHARE

1. *Where was the boy sitting?*
2. *Who will sit there now?*
3. *Why do you think the boy did this?*
4. *Name some people you respect.*

WHAT DO YOU SEE?

How do you know this is a bus? Why do you think it is not the inside of an airplane?

Shhh! Are You Listening?

Choosing to LISTEN

Shhh! Are you listening? Father is reading a story. He is not bowling with his friends. He is not at the office, working. He is not in the garage, fixing his car. He is here with you. You are the one person there with Father. That means you are special. It means the story he is reading is special too. Aren't you glad Father thinks you are this special? Aren't you glad he thinks it is important to read this story to you? Shhh! Are you listening?

WHAT DO YOU SEE?
Are Father and his boy good friends? How can you tell? What makes you think that Father is reading a story?

A TIME TO SHARE

1. *What is Father doing?*
2. *How important is this to him?*
3. *Why should the boy listen?*
4. *Why should you listen to your parents?*

My Kitty!

Choosing to be HELPFUL

Boys and girls like to help their parents. You like to help your mother and father, don't you? But fathers and mothers like to help their children too. Do you see what Father has done? The girl could not get the big ladder and put it up to the tree. She could not climb up to get her kitty. She needed her father to help her. Don't you think Father is glad he could help her? Don't you think she is saying "thank you"?

WHAT DO YOU SEE?
Is this winter? Why not? Do you think it may be summer? What do you see that tells you it is either spring, summer, or fall?

A TIME TO SHARE

1. *What did Father just do?*
2. *Why do you think the girl is happy?*
3. *How has Father or Mother helped you?*
4. *How have you helped Father or Mother?*

Something for You

Choosing to GIVE

Do you like to give good things? This boy and girl do. You know that because they look so happy. The lady in the wheelchair is happy too. She is always happy when someone comes to see her. That's because she can't walk. She must stay here in the hospital. Whenever she wants to talk to someone, she can't get in her car and go to their house. She must wait here, hoping that someone will come to see her. Now you know why she looks so happy. Boys and girls don't come to see her very much. And people don't often bring her nice gifts. Wouldn't you be happy if you were this lady? Wouldn't you be happy if you were this boy or girl?

WHAT DO YOU SEE?
How do you know this is a hospital or nursing home? Point to some things that tell you. How do you know these are gifts which the boy and girl are bringing?

A TIME TO SHARE

1. *What are the boy and girl doing?*
2. *Why do you think they are doing this?*
3. *In what ways do you like to give?*
4. *Why do you like to give gifts?*

What Did I Do?

Choosing to be RESPONSIBLE

"Oh, no! What did I do?" That's what this boy is asking himself. What did he do? Do you see what he left on his bed? That's his good suit. When he came home from Sunday School, he tossed it on his bed. You would never do that, would you? You would hang it neatly in your closet. That's what this boy should have done. Now he wishes that he had hung it up. Look what the boy's dog is doing. Perhaps now the boy will learn to be more responsible.

A TIME TO SHARE

1. *What should this boy have done?*
2. *What did he do?*
3. *Why should the boy be responsible?*
4. *In what ways can you be responsible?*

WHAT DO YOU SEE?

What room is this? How do you know? Point to some things that tell you this is the boy's room. Point to some things the boy should have hung up.

A Good Man

Choosing to RESPECT OTHERS
1 Samuel 26

That man on the ground should be ashamed of himself! He is a bad king. He has been trying to kill David. Now look at David. He won't let his friend kill the king. He respects the king. He believes that God made this man to be king. So David will not hurt him. And he will not let his friend hurt him. David is a good man, don't you think? What would you like to say to him?

A TIME TO SHARE

1. *What does David's friend want to do?*
2. *Why doesn't David let him?*
3. *Why does David respect the king?*
4. *Name three people you respect very much.*

WHAT DO YOU SEE?

Can you find the following: two spears, a shield, a waterpot, two swords, two helmets, the king, David, David's friend?

It's Hard to Wait

Choosing to be PATIENT

Do you smell that good food? Ummm! The turkey smells so good. So does the stuffing and the gravy. It's hard to wait for dinner, isn't it? That girl and boy are hungry. They have smelled the turkey roasting in the oven for a long time. They want to eat. But they can't eat until the food is cooked. Then they must wait for Mother and Father to put the food on the table. It's hard to wait. But that's how you learn to be patient.

A TIME TO SHARE

1. *What is this family going to do?*
2. *Why aren't the boy and girl eating now?*
3. *Why do they have to wait?*
4. *Why are they learning to be patient?*

WHAT DO YOU SEE?

Is this breakfast? How do you know it is not? How many plates do you see? Who will eat from each plate? How many dishes of food do you see? What do you think is in each one?

Which Way Should I Go?

Choosing to TRUST

"Which way should I go to the monkey house?" This boy is meeting his mother and father there. That's where they said they would be. The boy trusts his parents to be there. But he must trust someone to show him the way. Do you think he has chosen the right person to show him?

WHAT DO YOU SEE?

This man is showing the way to the monkey house. What do you see that tells you he is pointing in the right way? What do you see that tells you this man should know?

A TIME TO SHARE

1. *Who is this man? What work does he do?*
2. *Why should the boy trust the man?*
3. *Why does he trust his parents to be at the monkey house?*

It's Good to be Here

Choosing to be GOOD

These people certainly look happy, don't they? That's because they are in God's house. They sing together. They read their Bibles together. They pray together. And they listen to others tell about God. These are all good things to do, aren't they? God's house is a good place to do these good things. Today is a good time to be in God's house, doing these good things. That's why these people look happy. They are being good because they are doing good things.

A TIME TO SHARE

1. *What are these people doing?*
2. *Where are they?*
3. *Why do they look so happy?*
4. *Why are you happy when you do good things?*

WHAT DO YOU SEE?

Why do you think they are in church? What kind of window do you see? What kind of clothes are these people wearing? What kind of books do they have?

Who Should I Follow?

Choosing to FOLLOW

It's fun to watch the ducks. Look how fast they swim. Have you ever watched ducks swim by? The little ducks play follow the leader. They like to do this, especially when mother duck is the leader. They will not follow you. They will not follow your kitty or puppy. But they will follow the mother duck. That's because they trust her to take them to the right places. She will not take them where they will get hurt. That's good to remember, isn't it? What kind of people do you follow?

A TIME TO SHARE

1. *Who is the leader here?*
2. *Why do the little ducks follow her?*
3. *Name some people you trust.*
4. *Why do you trust these people?*

WHAT DO YOU SEE?

How many ducks can you find? Do you think the boy and girl are afraid of the ducks? How do you know?

What Are You Doing?

Choosing GOD'S WAY

Wouldn't you like to tell that boy something? Someone should. He is being foolish, isn't he? Look at that ladder. It is such a broken-down old ladder that he should not be on it. Do you see how far he is reaching for that apple? It would be easy for him to slip and fall. Wouldn't you like to tell that boy something? Why don't you?

A TIME TO SHARE

1. *What did you say to this boy?*
2. *Why?*
3. *What good choices have you made this week?*

WHAT DO YOU SEE?

How do you know this ladder is old and not safe?
What is the boy doing wrong?

Who Is First?

Choosing to PUT OTHERS FIRST
Mark 10:17-31

That rich man on his knees wants to know something important. He is asking Jesus how he can live forever in heaven. Jesus must have told him that he would have to accept Him as Saviour. But Jesus also wanted to know what was most important to this man. Was it his money? Was it Jesus? Was it others? "Would you give all your money away and follow Me?" Jesus asks. Jesus was asking the man if he would choose Jesus or money. The man was sad to hear this. He got up and walked away. The man wanted to go to heaven. But he would not put Jesus first. He loved his money more.

WHAT DO YOU SEE?
There are four men in this picture. Which one is Jesus? Which is the rich man? The other two are Jesus' friends. Point to them.

A TIME TO SHARE

1. *What did the rich man want?*
2. *What did Jesus say?*
3. *Which did he put first, Jesus or money?*
4. *Which do you want to put first? Why?*

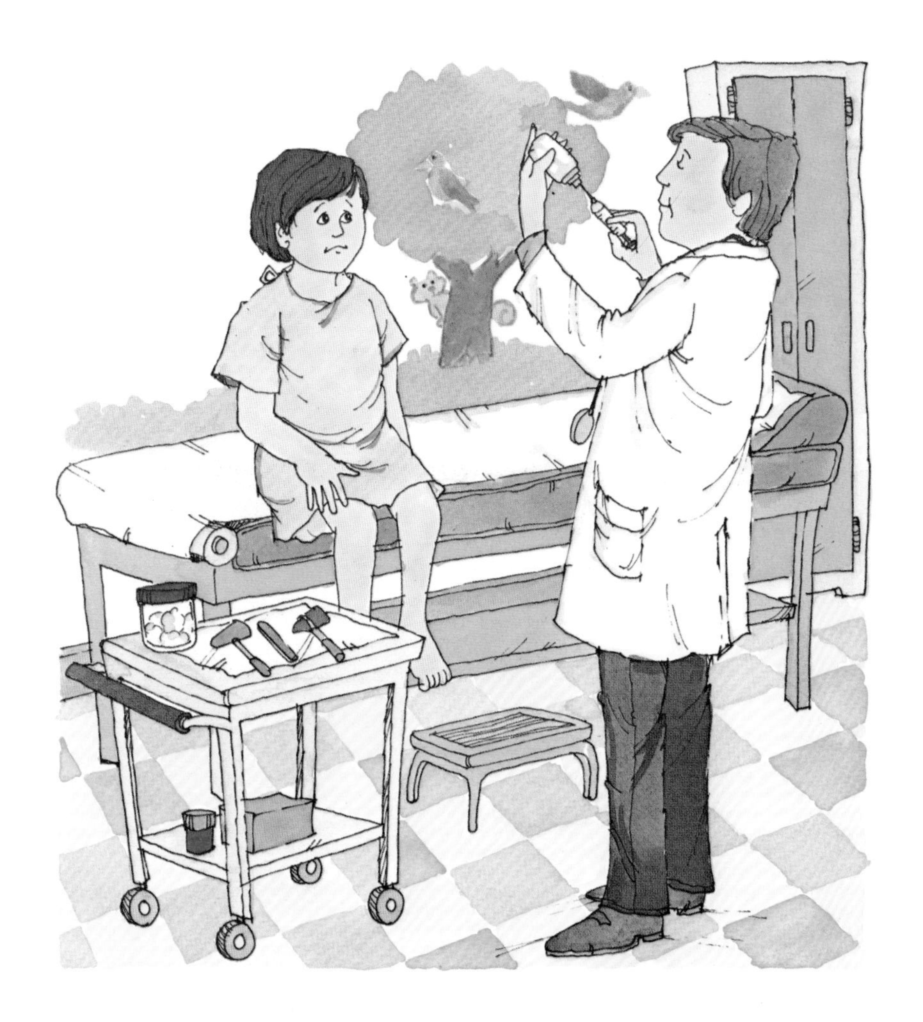

Will This Hurt?

Choosing to TRUST

Look at that long needle! This boy is going to get a shot. But he doesn't look very happy about it. He looks worried. The boy does not like the long needle. He is afraid it will hurt. That's all. He is not afraid that the doctor will give him something bad. He trusts the doctor to give him the right medicine. He knows the doctor will do what is best for him. We have to trust many people like this doctor, don't we?

WHAT DO YOU SEE?

Point to some things that show this is a doctor's office. Can you name some of them? Why do you think this man is the doctor?

A TIME TO SHARE

1. *Why does the boy look worried?*
2. *How does he trust the doctor?*
3. *Name some people you trust.*
4. *Why do you trust them?*

Someone to Love Me

Choosing to LOVE

Do you see the tear in Mother's eye? She is sad about something, isn't she? Perhaps someone said something to hurt her. Or she may be thinking about something sad. Whatever it is, she needs someone to love her. This boy is thoughtful. He knows Mother needs someone to love her. He knows that she needs him. That's why he has his arm around her. That's why he is saying some kind things to her. You know that Mother is glad for that, don't you?

WHAT DO YOU SEE?

Look at the boy's hands. Look at his eyes. How do they say, "I love you Mother"?

A TIME TO SHARE

1. *Why do you think Mother is crying?*
2. *Why does she need someone to love her?*
3. *What is the boy doing?*
4. *Have you told your mother "I love you"?*

My Parents Are My Friends

Choosing to be FRIENDLY

This boy had a good day. He wants to tell someone about it. Mother is glad too. She wants to hear about these good things. She wants to hear about things that weren't good too. Mother is a good listener. Sometimes Mother and the boy talk about many things. Sometimes Father and the boy talk. Mother and Father are the boy's parents. But they are also his friends. Good parents are good friends, aren't they?

A TIME TO SHARE

1. *What are Mother and the boy doing?*
2. *Why do they both look happy?*
3. *Why should parents and children be good friends?*
4. *Why should you and your parents be good friends?*

WHAT DO YOU SEE?

Where are the boy and his mother? How do you know? What time is this? How do you know?

Happy Birthday

Choosing to be HAPPY

Here is a happy family. Do you see the boy clapping his hands? It is not his birthday. It is his sister's birthday. But the boy is happy for her. He is glad that his sister can have a happy day. Father is happy for his girl too. And look how pleased Mother is to bring in this cake. She worked hard this afternoon to make it. She wants her girl to have a happy birthday. Don't you think this family is showing how to be happy?

WHAT DO YOU SEE?

How old is the birthday girl? How do you know? Why do you think each person is happy? Would you like to eat a piece of that birthday cake?

A TIME TO SHARE

1. *Why are these people happy?*
2. *Are they happier doing this together?*
3. *What do you think that girl is thinking?*
4. *Why should Jesus' friends be happy?*

Something I Don't Want to Do

Choosing to be PATIENT

Now there is something you don't want to do. Nobody likes to lie in bed at the hospital with a cast on a leg. You don't, do you? This boy doesn't like it. His mother and father don't like it either. They would much rather have their boy home with them. But the boy will have to wait until his leg is better. Then he can go home. So Mother and Father will have to wait too. Each of them will have to be patient. Don't you think so?

A TIME TO SHARE

1. *What is wrong with the boy?*
2. *What do you think happened to him?*
3. *Why must he be patient?*
4. *What would you like to say to him?*

WHAT DO YOU SEE?

Why do you think the boy is in a hospital? Point to someone who works in a hospital. What kind of work does she do? Point to something that tells you why the boy is in a hospital.

What Did I Say?

Choosing to be SORRY
Luke 22:54-62

That's Peter warming his hands by the fire. He is a good friend of Jesus. Peter told Jesus he would never say anything bad about Him. Good friends try not to say bad things about each other, don't they? But something happened here. Do you see Jesus back there? Some bad men have captured Him. Peter is afraid. What if someone captures him? "You're Jesus' friend, aren't you?" this lady is asking. Now Peter is really afraid. He is saying "NO!" Then Peter curses so the lady will think he is not Jesus' friend. But Jesus is listening. When Peter turns around he will see Jesus. He will be so sorry that he said those terrible things about his Friend.

A TIME TO SHARE

1. *What did the lady ask Peter?*
2. *Why did he say he was not Jesus' friend?*
3. *Are you ever ashamed to be Jesus' friend?*
4. *What do you say when people ask if you are?*

WHAT DO YOU SEE?

How many people can you find in this picture? Which is Peter? Which is the lady asking the question? Which is Jesus? Who are the others?

It's Time to Help Teacher

Choosing to be HELPFUL

Oh! Oh! That was an accident. Teacher didn't want to spill the crayons, but she did. We all have accidents, don't we? But what happens then? What will the boys and girls in this Sunday School class do? Will they laugh at the teacher? Or will someone help her? Do you see what that boy is doing on the floor? Is he laughing at the teacher? Is he helping her? This boy has learned to be helpful. Aren't you glad he has?

A TIME TO SHARE

1. *How did the crayons get on the floor?*
2. *Why not let Teacher pick up the crayons?*
3. *How is the boy being helpful?*
4. *What would Jesus think about this?*

WHAT DO YOU SEE?

Why do you think this is at Sunday School? Point to some things to show that it is. Do you see some boys and girls smiling? That means they are happy because the boy is helpful.

Sit Down

Choosing to OBEY

Here is a girl who is making a big mistake. Father told her and her brother, "Do not stand up in the canoe!" The girl heard Father. She knew what Father said. But she saw a beautiful bird up in a tree. "Look! Look!" the girl is shouting. She is excited. She is so excited that she forgets what Father said. She forgets to obey Father. We should never forget to obey our parents, should we? Don't you think Father is saying, "Sit down"? Don't you think Mother is saying, "Sit down"? Don't you think her brother is saying, "Sit down"? Don't you think you would like to say that too? Perhaps that would help the girl remember to obey.

WHAT DO YOU SEE?
Where are these people? Why should the girl not stand up in the canoe? What could happen?

A TIME TO SHARE

1. *What did Father tell this girl?*
2. *How is she not obeying?*
3. *Why does this not please Father?*
4. *Why does disobeying not please Jesus?*

Look What I'm Doing

Choosing to be RESPONSIBLE

Mother is smiling. That's because she is happy. She should be. Her girl is taking piano lessons. She must practice each day so that she will learn to play. But Mother does not want to nag her girl to practice. She wants her girl to practice without being told. That's why Mother is smiling. Her girl is practicing. Mother did not have to tell her. The girl is learning to be responsible. People are responsible when they do what they should without being told. Do you want to learn to be responsible?

A TIME TO SHARE

1. *Is the girl doing what she should?*
2. *Did she have to be told?*
3. *Is Mother doing what she should?*
4. *Did she have to be told?*

WHAT DO YOU SEE?

Where is Mother working? What is she doing? What time is it?

I'm Glad You Came

Choosing to be FRIENDLY

What a party! The cake is on the table and the ice cream is dished up. Three good friends are there and everything looks like fun. Then the doorbell rings. There is another good friend. She is late, but she is there. Look what the birthday girl is doing. She leaves the cake and ice cream. She leaves the three good friends for a minute. She is so happy to see her friend come to the party. Do you think the birthday girl is being friendly?

WHAT DO YOU SEE?
Point to some things that tell you this is a birthday party. How old is the birthday girl? How do you know?

A TIME TO SHARE

1. *Which is the birthday girl?*
2. *How do you know she is friendly?*
3. *Why do you think Mother is friendly too?*
4. *Think of some ways you can be friendly.*

Hungry Lions

Choosing to TRUST
Daniel 6

How would you like to be there with those hungry lions? Would you be afraid? What would you do? Daniel is God's friend. He likes to talk to God each day. But some bad men do not like Daniel. They want to kill him. So they had Daniel put here with these hungry lions. Do you think Daniel is afraid? What do you think Daniel is doing? He is asking God to take care of him. He trusts God to keep the lions from eating him. God will not let the lions hurt Daniel. He has shut their mouths. Now they cannot eat Daniel. God really loves Daniel, doesn't He?

WHAT DO YOU SEE?
Do you see a way for Daniel to get out of this room? There is no way. The bad people closed it. Do you see why the lions can't eat Daniel? Are their mouths open or closed?

A TIME TO SHARE

1. *Why is Daniel with these lions?*
2. *Who is keeping Daniel safe?*
3. *Why should Daniel trust God to do this?*
4. *How can you trust God to help you?*

What May I Do for You?

Choosing to be HELPFUL

Mother is busy baking a cake in the kitchen. Do you see her? She is making a cake so her family will have something good to eat. But it is hard to bake a cake and take care of the baby at the same time. The girl knows that. So she asks Mother, "What may I do for you?" Mother is happy that she asked. Now the girl can watch the baby and play with him. Mother can bake the cake. Later Mother and Father and the girl will have a good cake to eat. Do you think the girl is helping to make the cake in some way?

WHAT DO YOU SEE?

How many letters can you find on the blocks? What are the girl and the baby doing with these blocks? Why does this help Mother?

A TIME TO SHARE

1. *What is Mother doing?*
2. *What is the girl doing?*
3. *Why is this helping Mother?*
4. *Why will the girl be glad later?*

A Run Through the Meadow

Choosing to be HAPPY

How can you keep from being happy on a day like this? The sun is shining. The flowers are in bloom. And a beautiful butterfly is fluttering by. What a wonderful time to run through the meadow together! But some days are not like this. The sun isn't shining. There are no flowers or butterflies. Does that mean we should not be happy? Does that mean we should be grouchy and grumble at our friends and family? What do you think?

A TIME TO SHARE

1. *What are the girl and boy doing?*
2. *Do you like to be happy when things are bright and beautiful?*
3. *But will you be happy when things do not go so well? Why? Whom are you trying to please?*

WHAT DO YOU SEE?

Point to five things that tell you this is a happy day. Would you like to run through this meadow with the boy and girl?

How Much Do I Love You?

Choosing to show LOVE

Here is a dog that knows he is loved. The boy has his dinner ready for him. The girl is petting him and brushing his fur. Father smiles because he knows how much the boy and girl love their dog. He likes to see them show love to the dog. Father knows they are learning to show love to others too. Don't you think that kitten gets just as much love? She does! The boy and girl will soon get dinner for her and tell her how much they love her. Do you like to see this kind of love?

A TIME TO SHARE

1. *What is the girl doing?*
2. *What is the boy doing?*
3. *How do you know the girl and boy love their dog? Can you name some people or pets you love?*

WHAT DO YOU SEE?

Point to the dog. Point to the kitten. Point to two things that show that the boy and girl love their dog.

Look at That Water!

Choosing to TRUST

Exodus 14:1-29

Look at that water! Have you ever seen water piled up like that? God is doing it. His people are in trouble. Some soldiers are chasing them. But there is no place to go except through this sea. Moses asks God to pile up the waters so the people can go across and be safe. Moses trusts God. He believes God will help His people. Now you see what is happening. The people are crossing. They will be safe because Moses trusted God to help them. They will be safe because God piled up the water.

A TIME TO SHARE

1. *Why do these people need help?*
2. *How can God help them?*
3. *What does Moses trust God to do?*
4. *Why should you trust God to help you?*

WHAT DO YOU SEE?

Which man is Moses? He is holding out his staff and asking God for help. Who are those other people?

Plop!

Choosing to be RESPONSIBLE

Plop! Did you hear that candy wrapper fall into the basket? Do you see it falling? Mother sees it falling into the basket too. That's why she is smiling. She knows her boy is doing what he should. Father sees it falling into the basket. That's why he is smiling. He knows his boy is doing what he should. Sister sees it falling into the basket. She is smiling too, isn't she? That's because her brother is doing what he should. But look at that boy and girl going down the street. Are they doing what they should? Why not?

WHAT DO YOU SEE?

Do you see three candy bar wrappers? Point to each one. Which one is going where it should? Which wrapper makes you smile? Why? Why do the other two wrappers make you frown?

A TIME TO SHARE

1. *Where should paper and junk go when we are through with it?*
2. *Why not just throw it on the sidewalk?*
3. *Why are Mother and Father smiling?*
4. *Which boy and girl would Jesus smile at here? Why?*

What Are You Doing with That?

Choosing to be HONEST

Mother is busy at the checkout counter. Do you see her talking? The lady behind the counter is busy talking too. She and Mother have many things to say to each other. Perhaps that is why they do not see what Mother's little boy is doing. If they did, Mother would stop him. But the boy's sister sees what he is doing. She sees him taking a candy bar without paying for it. She sees him trying to steal the candy bar. Sister tells him to stop. She tells him that it is wrong to take something and not pay for it. Wouldn't you tell your brother or sister that if you were there?

A TIME TO SHARE

1. *Which one is Mother?*
2. *Why doesn't she see her little boy?*
3. *What would you like to tell the boy?*
4. *What does it mean to be honest?*

WHAT DO YOU SEE?

What kind of store is this? How do you know? What is Mother doing? What is the little boy doing? Why is that wrong? What do you think Sister is telling him?

Wait! Don't Start Yet!

Choosing to be PATIENT

It's not quite time to open gifts, is it? You can see Mother and Father still bringing gifts to put under the tree. But look at that little boy. He is starting to tear paper and pull ribbons. He doesn't want to wait! He wants to open the gifts now. He is not very patient. When we can wait to do things when we should, people say we are patient. When we don't want to wait, people say we are not patient. It's hard to be patient when it's almost time to open Christmas gifts, isn't it? But we should try.

WHAT DO YOU SEE?
What do you see that tells you this is Christmas? How many people are in this family? How many brothers? How many sisters? Why do you think this is a happy family?

A TIME TO SHARE

1. *What is the little boy doing?*
2. *Why should he not be doing this?*
3. *Why do you think he is not patient?*
4. *Why should you learn to be patient?*

Shhh!

Choosing to RESPECT OTHERS

"SHHH! Father is talking on the phone!" That's what you would like to say to this boy, isn't it? That's what his sister is saying! Poor Father. He is trying to talk to his friend, but he can hardly hear. Do you see him putting his hand over his ear to shut out the noise? The girl is showing respect to her father because she wants it to be quiet so he can hear. But the boy is not showing respect, is he? Wouldn't you like to tell that boy something? What would you say?

WHAT DO YOU SEE?

How do you know Father is talking with someone?
How do you know he is having a hard time hearing?
How do you know the girl wants things to be quiet?

A TIME TO SHARE

1. *What is that boy doing?*
2. *When is that wrong to do?*
3. *How should he show respect for Father?*

Will We Win?

Choosing to tell the TRUTH
1 Kings 22:1-40

Do you see the two kings? They are going to send soldiers into a battle. "Should we do it? Will we win?" the kings asked the men by the gate. "Yes, do it," the men said. "You will win." But these men did not ask God what they should say to the kings. God would have told them the truth. He would have told them the kings would not win. Because they did not ask for God's truth, they told the kings what they wanted to hear. But now the kings ask Micaiah. He is talking to the kings. He is saying, "No, you will not win." God told Micaiah the truth. So Micaiah told the kings the truth. Don't you think he was very brave? He could have been hurt!

WHAT DO YOU SEE?
Which men are the two kings? Which man is Micaiah? Which men did not tell the kings the truth? Which man did tell the truth?

A TIME TO SHARE
1. *What did the kings ask?*
2. *Who did not ask God for the truth? Why?*
3. *Who did find out what God said?*
4. *Why was Micaiah brave to tell the truth?*

Time for Dinner!

Choosing to OBEY

"Time for dinner!" You can almost hear this mother calling her two boys, can't you? One boy is hurrying toward the house already. He is obeying his mother. But look at the other boy in the sandbox. Is he obeying his mother? Do you think he wants to play for "just another minute"? Or perhaps he wants to build "just one more sand castle." How do you think his mother will feel when he does not come quickly, like his brother?

A TIME TO SHARE

1. *What is Mother saying?*
2. *Which boy is obeying his mother?*
3. *Why should we obey? Why not do what we want to do?*

WHAT DO YOU SEE?

Look at the two boys' faces. What do they tell you by the way they look? Which boy is pleasing his mother? Which is pleasing Jesus?

My Kind Helper

Choosing to be KIND

Do you like to help people? Do you like to be kind to them? What if these people can't do things for you? Do you see the lady in the wheelchair? She can't do much to help this neighbor girl, can she? She can't dust the girl's table or play ball with her. But that doesn't matter to this girl. She wants to be kind to the lady. She wants to help her even if the lady can't dust the girl's table or play ball with her. Do you think that is why the lady is smiling? Do you think that is why the girl is smiling too?

A TIME TO SHARE

1. *What is the girl doing?*
2. *Why do you think she is doing this?*
3. *What would you like to say to this girl?*
4. *What do you think Jesus would like to say?*

WHAT DO YOU SEE?

What do you see that tells you that this lady needs help? Why would it be hard for the lady to dust her own table and clean her own room?

Thank You for My House

Choosing to be THANKFUL

Do you see it snowing outside? It is a cold winter night. Who would want to sleep outside on a night like this? You wouldn't, would you? This boy would not want to sleep out in the snow either. He is thankful that God gave him a nice house where he can sleep. He is thankful God gave him a nice warm bed. He is thankful for a good mother and father who care for him. And he is thankful for the other good things God gave him. Now before he goes to bed, the boy wants to thank God for all these good things. Don't you think God is pleased that he is doing this? Don't you think his mother and father are pleased too?

A TIME TO SHARE

1. *Why is the boy on his knees?*
2. *What do you think he is saying?*
3. *Who is he talking to?*
4. *Why do you think his parents are pleased?*

WHAT DO YOU SEE?

What do you see that tells you this is winter? What tells you that the boy has a nice warm room? Point to some things that you think the boy is thankful to have in his room.

Who Is Doing the Dishes?

Choosing to be HELPFUL

What a nice girl to help Mother with the dishes! Mother is smiling. She is happy to have her girl with her in the kitchen. She is happy to have her girl help her. And look how the girl is smiling. Her face is even smiling back at her from the plate. That means she is helping her mother cheerfully. But look at the other girl in the living room. She is smiling, but not at her mother. While her sister helps with the dishes, this girl watches TV. What do you think of that? Does that make you feel good? Do you think it makes her sister feel good? Do you think it makes her mother feel good? Why not? What should she be doing? Are you happier when you are helpful?

WHAT DO YOU SEE?

What are Mother and the girl doing in the kitchen? Why do you think they are both smiling that way? What is the other girl doing? If you were the girl in the living room, what would you want to do? Why?

A TIME TO SHARE

1. *Which girl would you rather be like?*
2. *Why are you happier when you are helping?*
3. *What will you do when Mother needs help today?*
4. *Why will that make Mother happy?*

Follow Me

Choosing to FOLLOW
Luke 5:27-28

Levi has a good job. Each day he sits behind the table and takes money from people. Levi is a tax collector. People must pay their taxes to him. He gives some of it to the government. But he keeps as much money for himself as he can. Do you see who is talking with Levi? Jesus often stops here to talk. Levi listens to Jesus. He believes what Jesus says. Jesus is asking Levi to do something special today. "Follow Me!" Jesus tells Levi. Levi will follow Jesus. He will give up his good job. He will help Jesus do His work.

A TIME TO SHARE

1. *What kind of work does Levi do?*
2. *What does Jesus want Levi to do? Will he?*
3. *Levi had another name, Matthew. He wrote a book in your Bible with that name.*

WHAT DO YOU SEE?

How many different things can you find in this picture? Do you see: a boat, some coins, a bag of money, scrolls (Bible-time books), a Roman soldier, fruit?

I Will Not Get Angry

Choosing to CONTROL YOURSELF

How do you feel when someone makes fun of you? Do you want to punch that person on the nose? Do you get angry? This boy is trying to do his schoolwork. But two bigger boys are making fun of him. What do you think they may be saying? Do you think it would be easy for the boy to get angry? But he isn't. He keeps on doing his schoolwork. He does not look angry at all. That's because he is controlling himself. It's not easy. But you can do it too when someone makes fun of you. People will stop teasing if you don't get angry. Try it.

WHAT DO YOU SEE?
How many boys do you see? Which one is doing his schoolwork? Which ones are making fun of him? Look at the boy's face. Is he angry? Why not?

A TIME TO SHARE

1. *What would you like to say to those two naughty boys?*
2. *What would you like to say to the boy who won't get angry?*

It's Time to be Brave

Choosing to have COURAGE

Has anyone ever made fun of you? What did you do? What did you say? You can see what those two boys are doing. They are making fun of the boy and girl. The boy and girl are going to church. They are carrying their Bibles. Do you think the boys are making fun of them because of that? What do you think the boy and girl should do? Do you think the boy and girl are being brave?

WHAT DO YOU SEE?
Why do you think that is a church? Why do you think the boy and girl are going there? What are they carrying? What kind of clothes do they have on?

A TIME TO SHARE

1. *What are the two boys doing?*
2. *What should the boy and girl say?*
3. *Why should they not argue or fight?*
4. *How are the boy and girl showing they have courage?*

Thank You, God, for Water

Choosing to be THANKFUL

How do you get your water to drink? This boy and girl pump theirs at this old pump. The boy is getting a cup for the girl now. Do you see him pumping the water? He moves the handle up and down. This makes the water come out into the cup. The girl is thankful for the water. She is thirsty. She is thankful for her brother too. He is kind and polite. He is giving his sister water first. Then he will get some.

WHAT DO YOU SEE?
Is this in the city? How do you know that it is not? Where is it? Why do you think so?

A TIME TO SHARE

1. *How does the boy get the water?*
2. *For what is the girl thankful?*
3. *Are you thankful for water?*
4. *Are you thankful for those in your family?*

Look Out!

Choosing to be RESPONSIBLE

Look out! There's going to be an accident. That cat will knock over the glass of milk with its paw. Is this the cat's fault? Or did someone forget? The girl should never leave her glass that close to the edge of the table. She knows that her cat is mischievous. She knows her cat likes to do this kind of thing. But she left it there anyway. That is not being responsible, is it? Oh well, she can mop up the milk. The cat certainly won't do that, will he?

A TIME TO SHARE

1. *Why was this girl not responsible?*
2. *What should she have done?*
3. *What would you have done?*

WHAT DO YOU SEE?

What room do you think this is? Why do you think so? Why isn't it a bedroom? Why isn't it the living room?

Be Patient!

Choosing to be PATIENT

This boy wants to play ball. So does Father. But Father needs to finish the work he started. He told the boy that he would play as soon as he finished his work. Don't you think that is all right? But look at the boy. He is not being patient, is he? He stands there tossing his ball up and down. It's his way of saying to Father, "Hurry up!" But Father says something to the boy. Do you think he is saying, "Be patient"?

A TIME TO SHARE

1. *What does the boy want to do?*
2. *When will Father play with the boy?*
3. *Why should the boy be patient?*
4. *Why should you choose to be patient?*

WHAT DO YOU SEE?

What kind of work is Father doing? Do you think this will take him 10 more minutes or 10 more hours? Why do you think this?

A Happy Family

Choosing to be HAPPY
Mark 5:21-24, 35-43

Do you see the girl on the bed? She looks happy and healthy, doesn't she? But she wasn't healthy earlier today. She was a very sick girl. Her father thought Jesus could help her, so he went to find Him. But by the time Jesus came, the girl was dead. People were crying and making sad noises. Jesus made all the people leave the room except the girl's father and mother. Then Jesus spoke to the dead girl. "Get up!" He told her. Now look at the girl! That's why everyone is so happy. Aren't you happy for them?

A TIME TO SHARE

1. *Where did the girl's father go?*
2. *What did he want Jesus to do?*
3. *What did Jesus do for this family?*
4. *Name some things Jesus does for you.*

WHAT DO YOU SEE?

Which is the girl's mother? Which is the girl's father? What things can you find in this room?

Just One More

Choosing GOD'S WAY

Just one more thing! That's what this boy is thinking. But look what it is. The boy's sister knows that it is not wise to put a glass pitcher on top of the blocks. She knows that something bad might happen. You know that too, don't you? What would you like to tell this boy now? What would you like to say about making wise choices?

WHAT DO YOU SEE?
How many blocks can you count in this picture? Are there some blocks which the boy could still put on the tower? Where are they? How many more could he put on the tower?

A TIME TO SHARE

1. *What is that boy doing?*
2. *What is Sister trying to tell him?*
3. *What would you like to tell him?*
4. *Who can help you make wise choices?*

Who Will be My Helper

Choosing to be HELPFUL

Mother needs a helper. She wants to roll some yarn into a ball. It is hard to do this alone. "Who will be my helper?" Mother asks. "I will," says her girl. The girl is happy to be Mother's helper. She is not working very hard, is she? But she is doing something that Mother needs. Mother and her girl can talk and have fun while they work together. Mother says, "Thank you, helper." The girl smiles and says, "You're welcome. It's fun to be a helper."

A TIME TO SHARE

1. *What did Mother need?*
2. *Who wanted to be her helper?*
3. *Why will helping make the girl happy?*
4. *Why will it make Mother happy?*

WHAT DO YOU SEE?

How many balls of yarn can you find? Do you think the girl was a good helper for each of these? If you found six balls of yarn you found them all. Did you?

My Loyal Friend

Choosing to be LOYAL

Have you been sick lately? Did you have to stay in bed? If you did, you know how this boy feels. Staying in bed is no fun. Before long you get tired of TV or listening to the radio. You even get tired of books. If only someone could stay there with you all day and be your friend. Father can't stay all day. He has to work. Mother can't do it either. She has to do things too. But look at the loyal friend this boy has. Do you think this loyal friend will stay there with him?

WHAT DO YOU SEE?

How do you know this boy is sick? Point to some things that tell you. Aren't you glad he has a loyal friend to stay there with him?

A TIME TO SHARE

1. *Why is this dog lying there?*
2. *Why is the boy in bed?*
3. *Are you thankful for loyal friends?*
4. *Name some of your loyal friends.*

Please Forgive Me

Choosing to FORGIVE
Matthew 18:21-35

Do you see the man standing by the well? He owed a rich man a lot of money, but he couldn't pay it. So the rich man was going to put him in jail. That's what they did in Bible times. "Please forgive my debt," the man begged. The rich man felt sorry for him. He forgave his debt. But now look what is happening. That poor man between the soldiers owes this man a little money. "Please forgive my debt," the poor man begs. But this man will not forgive his debt. When the rich man hears about this, he will punish that wicked man. If we want others to forgive us, we must choose to forgive people too.

WHAT DO YOU SEE?
Do you see some spears? Can you find a sword? What can the poor man do against these strong soldiers?

A TIME TO SHARE

1. *Who owed a rich man a lot of money?*
2. *What did the rich man do?*
3. *What is happening here?*
4. *Why should you forgive others?*

My Warm, Cozy House

Choosing to be THANKFUL

Brrr. It is cold outside tonight. Do you see how everyone is bundled up? Mother looks cold, doesn't she? The boy and girl look cold, don't they? Father looks cold too. But look through the window. Do you see that the house is cozy and warm inside? Don't you think everyone will say "aaah" or "oooh" when they step inside and feel how nice and warm it is? Wouldn't you say something like that?

A TIME TO SHARE

1. *Are you thankful for a warm, cozy house?*
2. *Do you ever thank God for it?*
3. *Do you think this boy and girl thank God for their warm, cozy house?*

WHAT DO YOU SEE?

Point to the place where it is warm. Point to the place where it is cold. What would you say if you were this boy or girl now? What would you say when you step inside?

I'll Get the Mail for You

Choosing to be HELPFUL

"I'll get the mail for you." That's what this boy told his mother and father. It's quite a long walk from the house to the mailbox. The boy did not mind walking. He probably ran down here to get the mail. But it is easier for him to run down to the mailbox than for his parents to do it. That's why the boy said he would do it. Don't you think Mother and Father will say "thank you"?

A TIME TO SHARE

1. *What is the boy doing?*
2. *Why is he doing this?*
3. *Why do you like to be helpful?*
4. *Who does that please?*

WHAT DO YOU SEE?

Do you think this boy lives in the city? Why not? Where does he live? Why do you think this? Point to some things that look like a farm and name them.

Trusting My Leader

Choosing to FOLLOW

Someone has to go first. Usually it's the one who knows where to go. That's why Father is going first. He knows a good place to fish. The boy does not know where this is. He is happy to follow Father. He knows that Father will lead him to the right place. He can trust Father to take him there.

WHAT DO YOU SEE?
Where are the boy and his father? What are they going to do? How do you know?

A TIME TO SHARE

1. *Who is leading here? Why?*
2. *Why shouldn't the boy be the leader?*
3. *Why should we follow parents?*
4. *How can we follow Jesus? Why should we?*

My New Friend

Choosing to be GOOD

Luke 10:25-37

That man lying by the road is hurt. He was going down the road when some robbers jumped on him. They took his money. They beat him and hurt him. Then they left him lying by the road. One man came by. He was supposed to be a good man, but he did not stop to help. Another man came by. He also was supposed to be a good man, but he did not stop to help. Now look at this man who did stop. He is a Samaritan. The friends and neighbors of the man who is hurt do not think Samaritans are good people. But you see what he is doing, don't you? He is helping that man. He really is a good man, isn't he?

A TIME TO SHARE

1. *How did this man get hurt?*
2. *Who stopped to help him?*
3. *Can you name some people who are good to you?*
4. *Why does God want you to be good?*

WHAT DO YOU SEE?

Which man is hurt? How do you know this? Which man is helping him? What kind of animal is that up on the road? This good man will take the hurt man away on this donkey.

Happy Pickup Time

Choosing to be RESPONSIBLE

Have you ever had a happy pickup time? That's what this boy and girl are having. When it was playtime, they made a mess with their toys. You do that too, don't you? But there's a time to pick up toys and put them where they should go. That's pickup time. It's easy to make this a happy time too. Just pick up the toys without being told. That's why Mother is smiling. She did not have to tell the boy and girl to pick up their toys. They are doing it cheerfully, all by themselves.

WHAT DO YOU SEE?

How many toys can you name? Point to each one and tell what it is. Which toys are already picked up? Which toys will soon be picked up?

A TIME TO SHARE

1. *What are the boy and girl doing?*
2. *Why do they look happy?*
3. *Why does Mother look happy?*

Will You be My Friend?

Choosing to be FRIENDLY

Do you like to have friends? This girl with the valentine does. She knows she must be friendly if she wants friends. That's why she made this valentine. She is giving the valentine to the other girl. That shows she wants to be a friend. Do you think that is a good idea?

WHAT DO YOU SEE?

Why does the girl with the valentine look happy? Why does the other girl look happy? Which month of the year is this? How do you know?

A TIME TO SHARE

1. *What is the girl with the valentine doing?*
2. *Why is she doing this?*
3. *How can you have friends?*
4. *Who is your Best Friend?*

Will You be My Helper?

Choosing to be HELPFUL

Isn't it fun to go fishing with Father? But is it fun to put the worm on the hook? This boy doesn't think so. He thinks it is squishy. "Will you be my helper?" he asks Father. Father smiles. He is glad to be a good helper. Father doesn't mind a squishy worm. He will help his son put it on the hook. Do you like to put worms on a hook? Or do you need a helper for this too? Remember to say "thank you" when you have a helper. This boy remembered to say "thank you."

WHAT DO YOU SEE?

Where are Father and the boy? Are they on Main Street? Are they in the playground? Why do you think they are here?

A TIME TO SHARE

1. *Why does the boy need a helper?*
2. *How is Father helping?*
3. *What should you say when someone helps you?*
4. *How can you help someone today?*

Come, Look What I Found

Choosing to FOLLOW

"Come here!" Father found exactly what the family was looking for. This is a great picnic table in the park. It's under a big tree where the birds sing and the squirrels play. It's in a quiet corner of the park away from the crowds. Father is glad he found the table. As soon as he saw it, he called for his family to come here. Do you think Mother and the two happy children are glad to follow Father to this table? Do you think Father was a good leader?

A TIME TO SHARE

1. *Who found this picnic table?*
2. *How was Father a good leader?*
3. *Who were the followers?*
4. *Why did they follow Father here?*

WHAT DO YOU SEE?

What do you think this family will do here at the picnic table? Point to some things that tell you this is a picnic. Can you name some of them?

Pssst! Come Here!

Choosing to be a LEADER

"Pssst! Come here!" That's what those two boys are saying to our friend on the sidewalk. They want him to do something that he should not do. Have you ever had someone try to do that? Look at our friend. He doesn't really want to go with those boys. He knows they want him to do something wrong. This is a good time not to follow someone else. It is a good time to be a leader and say NO.

A TIME TO SHARE

1. *What are these two boys doing?*
2. *Do you think our friend will be sorry if he says yes to them?*
3. *Do you think he will be happy if he says no?*

WHAT DO YOU SEE?

Look at the hands. Do you see two hands that say "come over here"? Point to them. Why do you think these boys are on their way home from school?

Shhh! These Men Are Praying

Choosing to PUT OTHERS FIRST

Luke 18:9-14

This beautiful building is God's house. People come here to talk to God, just as you do at church and Sunday School. Here are two men now talking to God. You should hear them. That man near us is telling God how good he is. He is saying how important he is. That's his way of telling God, "I don't need You. I'm good enough now." He is putting himself first, and God next. But that other man is telling God how much he needs Him. He is putting God first, and himself last. Which prayer do you think God likes better?

A TIME TO SHARE

1. *Which man is putting himself before God?*
2. *How is he doing that?*
3. *Which man is putting God before himself?*
4. *How is he doing that?*

WHAT DO YOU SEE?

Point to some clothing that your father does not wear. What do these men have on their feet? On their heads? What are they wearing instead of suit, shirt, and tie?

Thank You for My Food

Choosing to be THANKFUL

Look at these people sitting under the tree. They have their eyes closed. Are they sleeping? What are they doing? This will be a fun day for this family. They have made a good picnic lunch. They have found a beautiful tree and a fun place to spread their blanket. Now they are ready to eat their good picnic lunch. But this family always does something first. They pray. They thank God for giving them the good food in the basket. Don't you think the food will taste better now?

WHAT DO YOU SEE?

Someone else is here at the picnic. Can you find a squirrel? Can you find a dog? Can you find a bird? God is there, but you can't find Him in the picture. That's because we can't see God, can we?

A TIME TO SHARE

1. *What are these people doing?*
2. *Who are they talking to?*
3. *Why do people thank God for their food?*
4. *Do you thank God for your food? Will you?*

Mine! Ours!

Choosing to SHARE

What a good boy that is! Look at him pull his younger brother on his sled. He is sharing his sled, isn't he? But that boy going down the hill is not sharing his! His poor sister is waiting. She hopes her brother will let her have a turn. But he doesn't. He keeps on sliding himself. What do you think the boy pulling the sled should say to him? What would you like to say to him? It's more fun to share, isn't it?

A TIME TO SHARE

1. *Which brother is sharing?*
2. *Which brother is not sharing?*
3. *Which brother do you think is happier? Why?*

WHAT DO YOU SEE?

Point to some things that tell you it is winter. What do the trees tell you? What does the clothing tell you? What does the snow tell you? What about the sleds?

Be Careful!

Choosing to TRUST

Oh! Oh! Be careful! You don't want to slip off that log, Father. Mother looks worried, doesn't she? The girl looks worried too. But Father does not look worried. He is sure he can walk across that log without falling. The boy does not look worried either. He trusts his father. He knows Father will not fall.

WHAT DO YOU SEE?

Who is Father carrying across the log? Is he carrying Mother? Is he carrying the girl? If Father falls, would Mother get hurt? Would the girl get hurt? Who would get hurt?

A TIME TO SHARE

1. *What is Father doing?*
2. *Why doesn't the boy look worried?*
3. *Name some people you trust.*

Oink!

Choosing to CONTROL YOURSELF

"Oink!" says the girl. She thinks her brother is being a little piggish. Mother and Father brought the boy and girl to this ice cream shop. Mother ordered a regular sundae. Father ordered a regular sundae. The girl ordered a regular sundae. But the boy wanted the biggest sundae he could get. He even fussed a little to get it. Mother and Father should have said, "No." But they didn't. Now he has the "oink" sundae. He will find out that it is too big. He will eat only some of it. The rest will be thrown away. Do you think the girl is right when she says "oink"?

WHAT DO YOU SEE?
Look at the boy's sundae. Is it as big as the other three together?

A TIME TO SHARE

1. *What is the boy eating?*
2. *Why do you think his sundae is too big?*
3. *What should Mother and Father have said when the boy wanted this sundae?*

Do You Know What She Did?

Choosing to tell the TRUTH

That girl with the crayons is not doing anything wrong, is she? She is minding her own business. But her friends over there are giggling and snickering. "Do you know what she did?" one asks the other. The other girl thinks it is funny, even though it is not true. Have you ever seen people do this? Why do you think it is wrong to say things like that? Who does it hurt?

A TIME TO SHARE

1. *What is the girl in the back saying?*
2. *Do you think it is true? Is that wrong?*
3. *What would you like to say to that girl?*

WHAT DO YOU SEE?

Why do you think this is at school? How many crayons do you see? What kind of book do you think the girl with the crayons has? Why do you think this?

I Was Wrong

Choosing to be SORRY
2 Samuel 19:16-23

Do you see that man on his knees? Shimei is kneeling down before King David. One day Shimei said some terrible things about his king. He even threw rocks at King David and called him a murderer. But now Shimei is sorry for the terrible things he said. He is afraid the king will kill him. "Please forgive me," he is begging. "Will you forget the terrible things I said?" The king's friends are angry at Shimei. They do not want to forgive him. But look at the king. He won't let these men hurt Shimei. "I forgive you," David tells Shimei. Don't you think David did what he should?

A TIME TO SHARE

1. *What did Shimei do that was wrong?*
2. *What does he want the king to do now?*
3. *What did King David do?*
4. *Why should we forgive people who ask?*

WHAT DO YOU SEE?

The king is about to cross a river. Can you find the river? Where is the raft he will use? Which man is Shimei? Which is the king?

Stop! Go! How Are You?

Choosing to be FRIENDLY

Look at that policeman. He blows his whistle and the cars stop. He blows it again and the cars go. He is an important person here. Someone might have an accident if he did not blow his whistle and hold out his hand. Those boys and girls think he is an important person. He makes the cars stop so that they can go across the street. It would be hard to do that without him. Do you see the boy and girl waving to him? They are friendly. The policeman is friendly too. But do you see the other boy and girl? They are not even looking at their friend, the policeman. They are not very friendly, are they? Perhaps they do not know what a good friend he is.

WHAT DO YOU SEE?
How do you know this man is a policeman? How do you know he is friendly?

A TIME TO SHARE

1. *What is the policeman doing?*
2. *Why is this important?*
3. *Which boy and girl are friendly?*
4. *What would you say to the others?*

Let's Clean Up the Mess

Choosing to be RESPONSIBLE

It's time to clean up the mess. When we eat we have dirty dishes and things. Someone has to clean up. Do you see the boy with the plate? He's doing his part. And look at the girl rinsing her dish. She's doing her part. But the other boy isn't doing his part. He would rather read. He thinks his brother and sister will clean up the mess. Do you think they should? Or should that boy learn to be responsible? Should he learn to clean up his own mess?

A TIME TO SHARE

1. *Who made the mess?*
2. *Who should clean up the mess?*
3. *Do you like to do your part?*
4. *How does that make you happy?*

WHAT DO YOU SEE?

Do you think the girl and boys are getting ready to eat, or have they eaten? How do you know? What room are they in? How do you know? How many dirty plates do you see? How many of the children ate?

Look at That Mess

Choosing to be HELPFUL

Look at that mess! You would never leave your room that way, would you? But this boy did. He did not make his bed. He did not fold his pajamas. He did not straighten his carpet. He did not pick up his toys. And look at his messy closet. Do you think that is why Mother looks so sad? She sees the boy playing outside. Couldn't he clean up that mess first? Wouldn't that make Mother happy? It would make the boy happy too. And it would make Jesus happy.

WHAT DO YOU SEE?
Tell what you would do with each messy thing that you see. When you're through, look at your room. Is there some mess there you want to clean up?

A TIME TO SHARE

1. *Who made the mess in this room?*
2. *Who should clean it up?*
3. *What would you like to tell the boy about being helpful?*

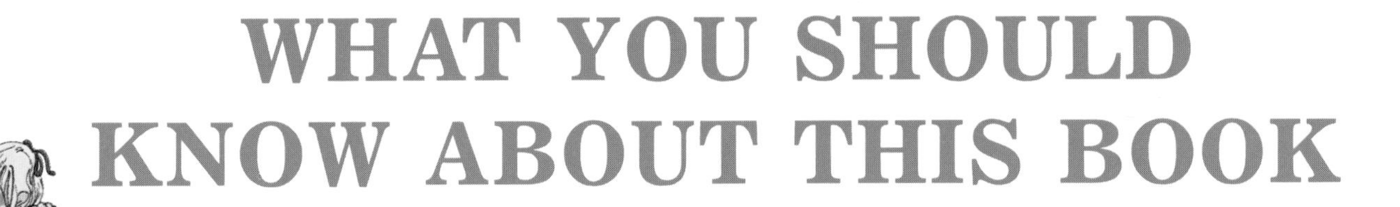

WHAT YOU SHOULD KNOW ABOUT THIS BOOK

CHOOSING GOD'S WAY TO SEE AND SHARE is a book about your child and the choices he or she must make. There are many such choices each day, often forcing your child to choose God's way or some other way. That "other way" may not be a way you or God would want the child to choose.

Choices and Your Child

As parents and teachers we try to help our children make the right choices in life. Wise children seek help from parents and teachers. But often you are not there when the child is confronted with that choice. He must choose alone.

It is at that moment that we hope we have done all we can to help the child make the right choice. This book is designed, not to make choices for your child, but to help your child learn how to make wise choices—choosing God's way.

This is not a teaching book as much as a learning book. It does not teach right choices as much as it helps the child learn how to make right choices. It does not tell the child what to do, but helps the child learn how to decide what is right and why. Thus it focuses less on the parent and teacher and more on the child as learner.

We cannot eliminate unwanted sources of choice, nor can we isolate children from situations where choice is demanded. Our children must grow up in a world in which it is expected that they will choose. As Christians, we hope that they will learn to choose God's way.

28 Basic Choices

This book focuses on 28 basic choices which we, including your child, face daily. These are listed alphabetically, by key word, in the table of contents, titled Choosing God's Way. These 28 choices are: (1) Choosing to CONTROL YOURSELF, (2) Choosing to have COURAGE, (3) Choosing to FOLLOW, (4) Choosing to FORGIVE, (5) Choosing to be FRIENDLY, (6) Choosing to GIVE, (7) Choosing GOD'S WAY, (8) Choosing to be GOOD, (9) Choosing to be HAPPY, (10) Choosing to be HELPFUL, (11) Choosing to be HONEST, (12) Choosing to be KIND, (13) Choosing to be a LEADER, (14) Choosing to LISTEN, (15) Choosing to show LOVE, (16) Choosing to be LOYAL, (17) Choosing to OBEY, (18) Choosing to be PATIENT, (19) Choosing to PRAY, (20) Choosing to PUT OTHERS FIRST, (21) Choosing to RESPECT OTHERS, (22) Choosing to be RESPONSIBLE, (23) Choosing to SHARE, (24) Choosing to be SORRY, (25) Choosing to be THANKFUL, (26) Choosing to TRUST, (27) Choosing to tell the TRUTH, and (28) Choosing to be UNSELFISH.

Vicarious Learning

What if you could be there with your child the next 100 or more times when he or she is faced with a difficult choice? What if you could quietly sit down and talk about it, and your child would listen? What if you could ask questions and discuss answers? What if you could do all this without interruption and in a pleasant place? None of these is likely! You won't be there for the next 100 times of choice. Nor will the circumstances be those described.

However, this book offers 174 situations, just like those which your child will face. Some are at school, others at home, and some in the back yard, and some in Bible situations. You ARE there, and you ARE talking these over with your child, and the child is listening. These 174 situations are true-to-life and your child can choose to make the same decision these people should have made, without actually being there. Vicarious learning is next best to learning in an actual situation.

The Read-to-Me Experience

Togetherness is built in the "read-to-me" experience. It is a two-way relationship, child reaching out to listen and learn as parent or teacher reaches out to share. No technology can ever replace the warmth of personal love and involvement. No television production or dramatization can ever replace the tenderness of adult and child interacting in this way.

This book is a read-to-me book. It is designed for you to read with your child. Thus it uses oral vocabulary rather than a child's "learning-to-read" restricted vocabulary. It also uses sentences and imagery associated with oral communication rather than those associated with beginning reading.

Tense Change

Sometimes you will find tense change deliberately within a page. This will happen especially with Bible situations, where the child is taken back into the Bible story so he can relive it. The event becomes a you-are-there experience.

This tense shift removes barriers to learning, such as time, culture, and lifestyle differences. Your child is part of this faraway situation as though it were an everyday situation on your street.

Tense shift is found less in the present-day situations, except to remove time restrictions and bring past, present, and future to focus in that one event.

Picture Reading

This book has 140 colorful paintings of everyday situations. These have been carefully chosen to represent the kinds of situations which confront your child over a period of time. You will "feel at home" as you encounter each one, for you have been in each too.

These 140 situations are ones often discussed in Sunday School and home devotions. You will find them compatible with your Sunday School lesson or home devotional material.

In addition, there are 34 Bible paintings of true-to-life situations. These are Bible events where honesty, truthfulness, love, and other basic choices are involved.

The primary thrust of the book is picture reading, in which you and the child read a picture instead of a story. There is no story to read, as we usually think of a story with plot and characters. Instead, the story unfolds as you look at the picture and "read" it together.

The reading acquaints the child with the situation, the people involved, and the choice they must make. Vicariously your child must choose with these people and learn from that how to choose in a real situation. Many times he will see in the same picture people making wise choices and some making foolish choices. These wise and foolish choices are contrasted so that your child will see how choosing God's way is making wise choices.

Picture reading is a visual experience. It helps your child see as you verbalize. It helps him enter into a true-to-life experience while sitting with you in your living room or Sunday School room.

Discovery Power

With each picture there is a small feature called WHAT DO YOU SEE? It helps your child develop "discovery power" by finding the little things in a picture that we ordinarily pass by in real-life situations. It also helps your child develop that "discovery power" by finding visual clues to the situation, especially clues related to the dynamics of choosing.

In WHAT DO YOU SEE? your child may be asked to study the faces of some people and guess what they are thinking or what they will say. He may discover what room of the house this is in, by pointing to objects associated with that room. He may be asked to find signs of fall or things that tell that this is bedtime instead of morning. He may discover what certain gestures mean and what certain clothing reveals.

This feature helps your child become more observant. You will find that he or she will begin to observe more of these kinds of things in real life. This will help your child become more creative and more imaginative.

Here are some examples that show how this feature encourages thought and imagination, observation and creativity:

1. On page 12, the picture shows a girl helping a lady pick up a package. The lady's arms are filled with packages so she really needs help. "Why should the girl smile?" helps your child think how helping makes the helper happy. "Why should the lady with the packages smile?" helps the child think how helping makes the person we help happy. And "Why should Mother smile?" helps the child think how helping a person in need pleases our parents.

2. On page 28 the picture shows a boy sleepily watching over his sick dog until late at night. The question "How do you know that it is late at night?" helps the child observe clues that the artist has put in to show the time. One question focuses the child's attention on the clock to show what time it is (this is an opportunity to help younger children learn more about telling time). Another question points to the boy's tired, sleepy eyes.

3. On page 89, the picture shows a family hiking in a woods. Questions ask for clues that this is a woods—such as the squirrel, leaves, a tree, a mushroom.

4. On page 123, the picture shows a family about to sit down to a turkey dinner. Questions ask if this is breakfast, and how the child knows that it is not. This encourages the child to distinguish between breakfast foods and dinner foods. It also asks the child how many plates are on the table and who will use each one (this helps younger children learn more about counting).

A Time to Share

A third feature on each page is called A TIME TO SHARE. There are usually three or four questions which encourage the child to talk about the situation which he has just "read." In this vicarious way, you and the child can talk about the choice at hand and what the person in the picture should do about it and why.

This sharing experience is a warm, wonderful opportunity for that two-way communication we value so much and find so seldom. It is your opportunity to think and talk with the child in the context of a choosing situation.

These questions perform many functions. Here are some examples:

1. Question 3, page 22 asks, "What special things do you like to do with Mother or Father?" This helps the child reflect upon those "together" experiences with parents that have been especially pleasant.

2. The picture on page 33 shows a boy and girl helping Father rake leaves while another boy sits in

a chair and reads. Question 1 asks what the boy in the chair is doing and Question 2 asks what he should be doing. This helps the child think about right and wrong activities. Question 3 asks, "Why do you think he would be happier if he helped Father and the others?" This helps the child think about associating happiness with helping.

3. Question 3 on page 60 asks about a pushy boy who is trying to get ahead of the other children as they board a school bus. It asks, "What would you like to say to him?" This helps the child verbalize what he might say if he or she were there in a similar

real-life situation. Question 4 focuses on what the boy is doing and asks, "Why does this not please Jesus?" This question helps the child think about the kinds of things Jesus expects of us and why wrong conduct is not pleasing to Him.

4. Some questions help the child think about the things we do to please God in daily life. For example, the picture on page 174 shows a family praying before they eat their picnic lunch. Question 1 asks what they are doing. This helps the child associate bowed heads or folded hands with prayer. Question 2 asks, "Who are they talking to?" which helps to focus prayer on the person of God. Question 3 asks, "Why do people thank God for their food?" It helps the child think about the reason for prayer. Question 4 applies the situation to the child's own life by asking, "Do you thank God for your food? Will you?"

Prayer Partnership

This book is a prayer partnership. We have prayed for its ministry in your child's life as we have written and developed it. You will have the opportunity to pray for your child as you share the book. And you may encourage your child to pray as a result of reading this book together.